THE GREAT ESTATES REGION
of the
HUDSON RIVER VALLEY

EDITED BY McKELDEN SMITH

GENEROUS SUPPORT PROVIDED BY
FURTHERMORE, THE PUBLICATION PROGRAM OF THE J. M. KAPLAN FUND
and
THE GREENWAY CONSERVANCY OF THE HUDSON RIVER VALLEY, INC.
THE FRANKLIN AND ELEANOR ROOSEVELT INSTITUTE
THE SAMUEL F. B. MORSE HISTORIC SITE
DUTCHESS COUNTY TOURISM

Contents

ISBN 0-912882-87-5   © Historic Hudson Valley Press, 1998

FOREWORD

*There was not one of them who did not think, and sometimes say, that his or her country-seat was the choicest spot
on the Hudson River; and that if there was nothing like it on the Hudson River, there was nothing like it in the world,
for there was no river to compare with the Hudson.*

—JULIA LIVINGSTON DELAFIELD, 1877

This book is your invitation to explore one of the most remarkable places in America—the Great Estates Region of the Hudson River Valley. Mrs. Delafield's charming remark about the country houses she knew and loved captures a bit of the enduring enthusiasm people have had for the Hudson Valley for over two centuries. We think you will come to believe that Mrs. Delafield's observation was not in the least overstated.

History proves that during the 19th century the Hudson River Valley was the center of artistic creativity in this country. Washington Irving, the first American to earn his living solely by writing, became an international celebrity, and *The Legend of Sleepy Hollow, Rip Van Winkle*, and other works are among the nation's enduring literary landmarks. Thomas Cole, Frederic Church, Albert Bierstadt, Jasper Cropsey, Asher B. Durand, and other great artists of the Hudson River School of painting established households here. Andrew Jackson Downing, Alexander Jackson Davis, and Calvert Vaux became the nation's leading taste-makers, revolutionizing thinking and practice in architecture and landscape through their own work and their influential publications. And later Richard Upjohn; McKim, Mead, and White; Richard Morris Hunt; Frederick Law Olmsted; William Welles Bosworth; Carrère & Hastings; Charles Platt; John Russell Pope; Beatrix Farrand; Ellen Biddle Shipman; and others made their mark.

Even by the mid-19th century, the Hudson Valley had become an exceptionally popular travel destination and remains so to this day. This guide takes you to ten important landmarks in the Great Estates Region, and we hope that eventually you will get to them all. Although you won't visit them chronologically, that's the way we have arranged them in this guide, because each individual landmark builds upon those preceding it in time. As you will quickly discover, the map of this part of the Hudson Valley is a complex web of family relationships, "a maze," quipped Eleanor Roosevelt, "from which there is no emerging."

Historic Hudson Valley is thrilled to be part of the Great Estates Region, where we preserve and interpret the magnificent Montgomery Place historic estate. This book, however, represents a partnership with two other like-minded organizations which recognize the benefits of working together to save important landmarks and to promote their enjoyment and appreciation by the public: the National Park Service and the New York State Office of Parks, Recreation and Historic Preservation. These two public organizations welcome you to six important properties between them. New York State presents Olana, Clermont, and Staatsburgh (now called the Mills Mansion); the National Park Service presents Hyde Park (known as the Vanderbilt mansion), Springwood, and Val-Kill. We are joined by The Samuel F. B. Morse Historic Site (Locust Grove) and Wilderstein Preservation, both private endeavors, and by the National Archives and Records Administration, which operates the FDR Presidential Library in Hyde Park.

As the bibliography at the end of this guide clearly shows, much has been written about the history and architecture of the Hudson Valley, but, incredibly, this is the only publication in print which pulls the story of the landmarks of the Great Estates Region together in one place. Undoubtedly this is because we are six separate organizations. This guide shows we have *everything* in common.

Preparation of this guidebook—a great effort involving dozens of individuals listed in the acknowledgments—has in particular benefited immensely from the support of Joan K. Davidson and Furthermore, the publication program of the J. M. Kaplan Fund. We are grateful for additional support of Dutchess County Tourism, the Greenway Conservancy of the Hudson River Valley, Inc., the Samuel F. B. Morse Historic Site, the Franklin and Eleanor Roosevelt Institute, and the FDR Library in Hyde Park. Without their support this guide would not exist.

John H. Dobkin
President, Historic Hudson Valley

INTRODUCTION

There is no part of the Union where the taste in Landscape Gardening is so far advanced,
as on the middle portion of the Hudson.

— A. J. DOWNING

With this pronouncement in his best-selling book of 1844, *A Treatise on the Theory and Practice of Landscape Gardening*, the influential taste-maker Andrew Jackson Downing confirmed the cultural primacy of the river-front treated in this guide. Whether citing Clermont as "the show place of the last age" or praising Montgomery Place as "rarely surpassed in any country," Downing's celebration of the country seats in this region—and indeed his direct or indirect contributions to their embellishment—helped to fix forever in the popular mind the special character and significance of these properties.

Their importance, of course, is not limited to Romantic-era topography, horticulture and architecture — the focus of Downing's interest. Then and now, these "places" (to use the term commonly employed by the owning families) illustrate numerous other themes in the history of the Hudson Valley and the nation during the past 300 years. Remarkably, this "emerald necklace" stretching between the cities of Poughkeepsie and Hudson, New York, along the east bank of the historic estuary, survives largely intact a century and a half since publication of Downing's statement.

Indeed, in 1990 the Secretary of the Interior formally designated 18 miles of this river-front as the Hudson River National Historic Landmark District, at 22,000 acres one of the largest and most complex such districts in the nation. The Landmark District, which both comprises the State's first designated Scenic Area and provides a notable feature of the State's Hudson River Greenway and the Congressionally specified National Heritage Area, highlights some forty country seats established between 1790 and 1940 that derive chiefly from the great land grants made to Robert Livingston, Pieter Schuyler and Henry Beekman in the late 17th and early 18th centuries. Most of these seats came into being at the behest of one or another of the ten remarkable children of Margaret Beekman Livingston or of one of his or her progeny, and a few are still in the possession of direct

OPPOSITE: Margaret Beekman Livingston (1724–1800). Gilbert Stuart, circa 1794. Oil on canvas, 36" x 28". Clermont State Historic Site, New York State Office of Parks, Recreation, and Historic Preservation. This is one of at least four portraits of Margaret Beekman Livingston—one of which hangs at Montgomery Place—painted by Stuart, who visited Clermont in 1794. (Stuart also painted Chancellor Livingston and other family members.) Mrs. Livingston's ten surviving children and their descendants built over three *dozen* notable houses on the Hudson River between 1790 and 1940. For example, Margaret's oldest daughter, Janet, built nearby Montgomery Place. Margaret's daughter Gertrude and Gertrude's husband, Gen. Morgan Lewis, built the first Staatsburgh. Margaret herself is credited with rebuilding Clermont after it had been burned by the British.

RIGHT: Chancellor Livingston's bookplate depicts the Livingston's Scottish arms: in the first and fourth quarterings are three gilliflowers for Livingston; in the third are six billets, for Callendar. The second quartering contains the Hepburn arms. The arms connect the Livingston family to noble Scottish houses, both correctly (Callendar) and incorrectly (Hepburn). The Latin motto *Spero Meliora* ("I hope for better things") replaced the previous motto in the late 17th century. The crest featuring a ship under full sail was adopted about 1785 by William Livingston (1723–1790), a distinguished cousin of the Chancellor and first Governor of New Jersey. In the Chancellor's bookplate the arms are surrounded by books and objects suggesting travel, learning, and civic honors.

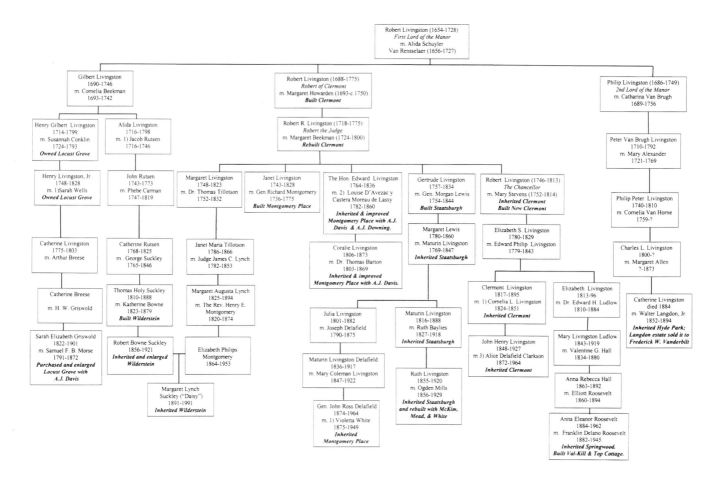

Selected branches of the Livingston family tree. This chart shows the relationship among the branches of the Livingston family and the landmarks showcased in this book. (Remarkably, only Olana has no direct Livingston connection.) The Livingston family tree is also interesting because it shows the interconnectedness of the family with others of importance in New York history; for example the Van Rensselaer, Beekman, Lewis, Roosevelt, Mills, and Schuyler families appear in just this tiny section of the tree. Chart created by J. Winthrop Aldrich and Historic Hudson Valley, 1998.

descendants. The district also includes five hamlets and villages that have close historical ties with the nearby seats, and with commerce related to river and railroad. The vernacular dwellings and commercial structures found in these communities greatly enrich the overall architectural diversity and social history of the district.

The survival of these historical gems and their settings is not by chance or luck alone. Landowners and heirs, private citizens, local and national organizations, charitable foundations, scholars, journalists, and town, state and federal officials have all played valuable initiating or supportive roles, especially during the past quarter century. They have done so in part because the most visible of these landmarks—those that are discussed in this guide—compose a critical mass within 35 miles of each other, luring the heritage tourist from the four corners of the globe. Yet even absent the profit motive and the boon to the region's economy, the preservation of these astonishing resources would be the

proper course, advancing the public interest by securing an important part of our cultural patrimony.

We especially honor the leaders of government agencies who pioneered the acquisition and rehabilitation of historic sites here at a time when it was rarely done: the National Park Service at Hyde Park in the 1940s, and, in the 1930s and 1960s the Taconic State Park Commission (now known as the State Office of Parks, Recreation, and Historic Preservation) at Staatsburg, Clermont, and Olana. They had the vision and the will then; they have it still. As faithful stewards on behalf of an appreciative public, they are the true heirs of those who preceded them at these landmark places.

Mention must also be made of the efforts of Hudson River Heritage, Inc., in documenting, publicizing and fostering the protection of this region, and of Scenic Hudson, Inc., in doing the same with a special focus on the preservation of scenic lands near the River. More will always need to be done, as buildings age, landscapes evolve, and economic pressures mount. Subdivision and development of large tracts, commercial development of road frontages, the shift of the market focus from the historic village to the shopping plaza invading a former agricultural setting, all take their toll on our sense of place and on the quality of the visitor's experience. It is everyone's good fortune that this problem is now generally acknowledged and that mechanisms such as conservation easements, historic preservation investment tax credits, and improved town planning and zoning are gradually coming into wider use. Moreover, within the past fifteen years Wilderstein, Montgomery Place, the Tivoli Bays State Nature Preserve, and Scenic Hudson's Poets' Walk Park have all become acclaimed, publicly accessible resources. Scenic roads and historic tourways have been designated, and public hiking trails established.

Two great objectives to be achieved now are the continuation of viable farming and the maintenance of farmland, and the reestablishment of significant passenger boat travel between New York City and Albany, with local landings and on-shore transportation refitted to accommodate such operations. The houses discussed here were designed and situated to permit the River to be seen — and to be seen from the River. But, sadly, nowadays the water-borne are not there to do the seeing.

While this guide eloquently summarizes the significance of properties that now operate as museums, their geographical and social context continues largely to be that of privately owned big country places and of hamlets — traditional uses of the land and community life that are no less deserving of respect and preservation than the superb collections in the nearby house museums.

As the critic John Russell observed about this district in a *New York Times* article several years ago, "The landscape has that largeness of cut, that breadth of shoulder and that comfortable shagginess that comes about when acres have stayed together under the same ownership for the best part of two hundred years."

How is it, then, that this remarkable concentration of distinguished country houses and related landscaped grounds and farms evolved here and endured? A short answer is found in the dual tendency of Livingstons to adhere to each other and to adhere to their land. To say they were (and are) extreme in these matters is no exaggeration. A descendant who owned one of the more notable places, at the tender age of 29 in 1900, was able to write about her property as follows:

The place from the beginning has been beloved; by those who owned it, by those who might have owned it, and by many who have been only occasional guests. Almost every story told me (about earlier generations) begins or ends: "her affection for the place was immoderate," or "he did not like to be anywhere else." . . . I myself am capable of praying that he who comes to hold the place without love may be unhappy in his life and death.

A hundred years earlier the Polish patriot Julian Niemcewicz recorded his impressions after a visit to Clermont in 1798:

. . .Because they {the Livingstons} marry among themselves, their estates are increased rather than broken up. The mother of the Chancellor, heiress to the rich Beekman family, brought more than one hundred thousand acres of land to the Livingston estate. . . . The most attractive conversation for these lovers of republican equality is about the ancient lineage of their family, about the arms of the

Edgewater is a handsome temple-form villa built in 1821–24 by John R. Livingston, not far from Montgomery Place, as a wedding present for his daughter. The aptly named Edgewater is particularly well positioned to be seen from the river. It was so easily identifiable that it became a navigational landmark. Engraving from the Atlantic Local Coast Pilot (1880).

Livingstons, about the ramifications of the family and the extent of their relationships, etc. . . . . One of the greatest advantages of living here on this beautiful river is the pleasant neighbors who are in good accord. The trunk of the Livingston family is wide; it spreads its branches in all directions. All these people are well-to-do, polite, related, closely-knit in friendships and sentiment.

From these recollections one receives a clear notion of a powerful ethos at work. The interconnectedness of the Livingston family and its "hiving" like bees on ancestral land is further illustrated in the family chart. Every one of the places discussed in the guide with the exception of Olana has been owned at some point by Livingston kin, and even at Olana there is a link, as a direct descendant of the last Lord of the Manor is married to a great-granddaughter of Frederic Church and they reside at Oak Hill, an important Livingston house within sight of Olana.

The intensity of this hereditary feeling for the land summons up the image of Antaeus, the giant in Greek mythology whose invincible strength was renewed every time he had physical contact with his native soil. This mystical attachment to place, like the family's preoccupation with Livingston genealogy, lore and artifacts, has endured for a dozen generations; while not uncommon among landed families in Britain and on the continent of Europe, it has been something of a rarity in this country. The historical context is provided by the scholarly authors of a leading textbook on property law:

In Old England the ancestral estate, not commerce, was normally the basis of the family fortune. It was also the focus of family pride. These factors provided the motivation for attempts to keep the land in the family as long as the family lasted; and the estate tail was the basic instrumentality designed for that purpose. By way of contrast we in America have, generally speaking, no such attachment to the land. . . . There are a few exceptional cases of attachment to the land—in the Old South, in New York's Dutchess County—but not many.

Indeed even this century's pre-eminent "friend of the forgotten man" was imbued with these attachments and these customs. A survey of the FDR Library and of his life will amply demonstrate that the President was by instinct a collector, local historian, and antiquarian intimately familiar with family annals – his own and those of his Livingston wife. FDR's study and employment of Dutch colonial architecture were manifestations of this habit of mind.

The Livingstons were not without grounds for pride in the family's accomplishments as early colonial administrators and private entrepreneurs, and later as political and military leaders in the patriot cause and during the subsequent Federal era. Some of these eminent figures, most notably Chancellor Robert R. Livingston of Clermont, a dean of the American Enlightenment, Edward Livingston of Montgomery Place, and Eleanor Roosevelt of Val-Kill are discussed more fully in the pages that follow. What deserves emphasis is the inclination of so many in this family, down to the present time, to enter public service or to make a mark in public affairs.

A recent flowering of the old commitment to land and public service is found in the remarkable series of acts of land philanthropy initiated by Livingston descendants in this district during the past sixty-five years. Of the ten properties discussed in this guide, only Locust Grove, Hyde Park, Val-Kill, and Olana have not involved gifts or partial gifts by Livingstons. In addition, six other major gifts of interests in land in this area may be credited to Livingston descendants.

With the inevitable passing of the political and economic dominance of the Livingstons in the Hudson Valley in the middle of the 19th century, the quieter, more private life of a cultivated squire and manager of investments befell many in the later generations of the family. Theirs was a leisure with dignity, and a sense of obligation to the well-being of the community.

> Happy the man, whose wish and care
> A few paternal acres bound,
> Content to breathe his native air,
> In his own ground.

These lines from Alexander Pope's *Ode on Solitude* (1727) were written out in a recently discovered early 19th century notebook, probably belonging to Montgomery Livingston, the artist grandson of Chancellor Livingston.

Support of the community's religious life was profoundly important to these land-owners and reflected a journey across the generations from Dutch Reformed worship to Episcopalian, with (for some) a devout detour to Methodism in the 19th century. (The families of Frederic Church and Samuel Morse were Presbyterian.) Churches were erected and endowed; vestryman Robert B. Suckley was a co-donor of the site for his parish's new church building in Rhinebeck; and Franklin D. Roosevelt, John Henry Livingston, and Ogden Mills each served for decades as wardens or vestrymen of their respective Episcopal parishes.

While the "old money" was sustaining an ever more modest style of living for some property owners, others were renewing their prospects by marrying into "new money" such as that of the Millses, the Mortons, and the Astors.

View from Montgomery Place looking northwest. Artist unknown (Herne?), 1854, oil on panel, 18½" by 12". Rokeby Collection. The view, perhaps partly embellished by the artist, captures the pastoral landscape idealized in mid-century by artists, writers, landscape gardeners, and patrons. The newly invading railroad is tactfully not shown.

Ownership of the places in this neighborhood by those whose social and business lives were centered in Manhattan was made more convenient and attractive by the coming of all-season rail service. House guests could come and go with ease, and the busy "man of affairs" was no longer isolated from his office. This development did much to remove the sense of proud remoteness and rustic self-reliance that had been so characteristic of prior generations here.

The life at the Hyde Park of Frederick Vanderbilt and at the Staatsburgh of Ogden and Ruth Mills a century ago was a far cry from the Suckleys' world at Wilderstein. The Gilded Age plutocrats, however warmly they may have felt toward their Hudson River seats, used them only seasonally and had a number of other residences in very different settings to which they were also attached; and further insulating each from property management cares was a large staff of employees. But long after the Vanderbilts and Millses had departed from the scene the Suckleys were still quietly at home, patching their roof, pouring their tea, and admiring their view.

And what memorable views these places had and still have! This is what the Swedish travel writer Fredrika Bremer recounts about a visit with the Downings to Blithewood, next door to Montgomery Place, in 1849:

The banks of the river, which were scattered with houses, appeared rich and well cultivated. There were no castles, no ruins here, but often very tasteful houses, with terraces and orchards, whole parks of peach trees. The only historical legends of these shores are a few traditions of wars with the Indians. I did not seem to miss the ruins and the legends of the Rhine. I like these fresh new scenes, which have a vast future. We have ruins enough in the old world.

. . .When, however, in the evening . . . and accompanied by the silent Mr. Downing, I wandered quietly beside the glorious, calm river, and contemplated the masses of light and soft, velvet-like shadow which lay on the majestic Catskill Mountains, behind which the sun sank in cloudless splendor; then did the heart expand itself, and breathe freely in that sublime and glorious landscape.

Many of the leading practitioners—indeed the originators—of landscape design in this country made and left their mark on properties here. Shaping the vistas of river and distant mountains was a key element in this artistic work: Parmentier at Hyde Park, Downing at Montgomery Place, Vaux at Wilderstein, Church at Olana, and elsewhere in the district Ehlers, Olmsted & Vaux, Olmsted Bros., and Platt. In this century talented amateur horticulturists such as Violetta Delafield at Montgomery Place and Alice Livingston at Clermont created significant gardens of their own.

Essential to many of these landscape treatments was the role of an idealized pastoral, agrarian scene in the middle distance—visually picturesque with trees planted to shape vistas, but not so close as to permit livestock or harvesting to disrupt the tranquillity of the observer or suggest an actual dependence on farm income. In 1853 the essayist Nathaniel Parker Willis made these amusing observations about the trend:

"The opening down the middle" of the Empire State's robe of agriculture will soon be edged with velvet—A "class who can afford to let the trees grow" is getting possession of the Hudson. . . .With bare fields fast changing into wooded lawn, the rocky wastes into groves, the angular farmhouses into shaded villas, and the naked uplands into waving forests, our great thoroughfare will soon be seen (as it has not been for many years) in something like its natural beauty. It takes very handsome men and mountains to look well bald.

These "shaded villas" were designed by the leading architects of the age: Alexander Jackson Davis at Montgomery Place and Locust Grove, Frederic Church, Calvert Vaux and Richard Morris Hunt at Olana, Charles McKim at Hyde Park and Stanford White at Staatsburgh. Elsewhere in the neighborhood the work of Frederick C. Withers, Richard Upjohn, Potter Brothers, Whitney Warren, Charles A. Platt, Delano & Aldrich, and John Russell Pope is to be seen, along with other commissions by Davis, Vaux, Hunt and White. It is truly an all-star cast; yet some of the most memorable buildings are the products of little-known designers or unidentified builders.

This is a reminder of the role of patronage in the arts. An architect or landscape gardener must have a client before there can be a product. Patronage of the arts and sciences was important in the life of Chancellor Livingston and many of the others whose properties are under discussion. Nevertheless, while Montgomery Livingston of Clermont, Frederic Church, and Samuel Morse were all 19th-century painters, it is not evident that they enjoyed the patronage of their neighbors and relatives, who were more likely buying European paintings. Important as the Hudson River School of landscape painting was in the development and appreciation of American art, it seems likely that the local gentry preferred their views of the Catskills and the Hudson to be "from the hand of the Artist Inimitable," in Christopher Smart's phrase.

The Point, as this important villa was called, was designed for Lydig Monson Hoyt by Calvert Vaux and built 1852–58 on a site just south of Staatsburgh. Vaux published its design in his style-book *Villa and Cottage Architecture* (1857.) Currently owned by the state of New York, efforts are underway to ensure the preservation and sympathetic use of this landmark. Photo: New York State Office of Parks, Recreation, and Historic Preservation.

Two 19th-century iceboats on the Hudson, not far from Wilderstein and the Kingston lighthouse (background, right). On the left is *The Vixen*, once owned by FDR's uncle John A. Roosevelt. The other is *The Rip Van Winkle*, owned by Winthrop Aldrich and his family. Photo: Thomas Brener, the Museum of Rhinebeck History, 1981.

The Hudson River was vital for transport during the ice-free months and before the advent of the Hudson River Railroad in 1851. Sloops and, after 1807, steamboats and barges carried passengers, moved produce down-river to market and shipped manufactured goods upriver to consumers. It was also a focus of sport, most notably in the decades following the Civil War with the development of competitive ice yachting, a winter activity still practiced, with many magnificent 19th century "stern-steerer" iceboats in commission more than a century after they were first sailed.

The River, sorely beset by pollution and virtual abandonment in recent decades, has at last found its champions, and its health is rebounding. The Hudson's astonishing biological diversity as a tidal habitat and ecosystem would come as no surprise to Theodore Roosevelt, whose parents rented the property adjoining Montgomery Place in the summer of 1868. The nine-year-old future President kept his first diary that summer, documenting the start of his lifelong commit-ment to natural history and conservation as he methodically explored the River's wooded banks and marshes.

Truly, the River is the great silken thread on which are strung emeralds of land and landmark. It is the unifying element in the chronicle of these country seats and their families, as surely as it is the common feature in the views the places command. Just as the future of this great natural treasure is brightening, so too is the outlook for the great cultural treasure which hugs its east bank—the places described so concisely and invitingly in this book, and all the places in between. Like the Hudson, they beckon, and with gladness we respond.

– J. Winthrop Aldrich

J. Winthrop Aldrich, a descendant of the First Lord of the Manor, is a leader in the effort to preserve the great estates region in the Hudson River Valley. He is a co-owner of a historic river-front place to which his family has held title for eleven generations.

West (river) front. The high-pitched slate roof replaced the original low-hipped roof in 1874. The Colonial Revival door surround was part of the 1920s renovation. Photo: Richard Pileggi, 1997, for Historic Hudson Valley.

CLERMONT

CLERMONT STATE HISTORIC SITE * GERMANTOWN

*The Spirit of Clermont is one of love, loyalty, generosity, and right living and one cannot remain within its walls
and harbor thoughts contrary to that spirit—nor live a life unimbued by its enobling influence.*

— PEYTON MILLER, 1927, A FREQUENT GUEST AT CLERMONT

The Livingston family's Clermont, the oldest of the mid-Hudson estates, has a romantic history evoked by its expansive grounds, buildings, surviving gardens, and unspoiled natural beauty. It was at Clermont that the Livingston family established the first of the great estates which formed the culture and character of the mid-Hudson River Valley.

In 1686, Robert Livingston (1654–1728), a talented and ambitious Scot, secured a royal patent for 160,000 acres in what is now Columbia County, New York; eventually the Livingston family landholdings approached a million acres. As First Lord of Livingston Manor, Robert Livingston created a distinguished land-owning and political dynasty that lasted well into the 19th century. The Livingston family also evolved into a powerful *social* dynasty, still in existence, reinforced by frequent intermarriage and the family's accelerating interest in heritage and genealogy. (For a glimpse of the family's complex and fascinating genealogy, please turn to the introduction to this guidebook.)

Robert Livingston's grandson Robert R. Livingston ("Robert the Judge," 1718–1775) married a cousin, the heiress Margaret Beekman (1724–1800); by the mid-18th century he succeeded to the Clermont estate and the early 18th-century house built there by his father. Their eldest son Robert R. Livingston, Jr. (1746–1813), later known as Chancellor Livingston, also built a house at Clermont, naming it Belvedere.

In 1777 the British burned both Clermont and Belvedere. Almost immediately, the widowed Margaret Beekman Livingston began rebuilding Clermont atop the charred foundation of the earlier house, aided by her African-American slaves and by tenants requisitioned from the State Militia. The following year Margaret's son Robert reported that

. . .I have dipped my hands in mortar in spite of the want of leisure, of materials, & workmen. I have such strong attachments to Clermont that I find myself at home nowhere else—And am now laying out as much in building a paltry farm house as would formerly have built me a palace.

In 1781, Margaret Livingston entertained George and Martha Washington in her new house, which stands today.

The drawing room, in which George and Martha Washington were received in 1781, reflects seven generations of occupancy. The mid 18th-century Chippendale-style chair, silhouetted by the window, is American; the Hepplewhite-style shield-back chair (c.1795) is English. Reflected in a mirror is a portrait (c. 1795), possibly by Charles Willson Peale, of General Richard Montgomery, who married Janet Livingston at Clermont in 1773. (There is another version of the same portrait at Montgomery Place.) The chandelier and the mantel clock may have been purchased by Chancellor Livingston in Paris when he was minister to France (1801–1805). The clock, which depicts the first flight of a hydrogen balloon, reflects the Chancellor's fascination with transportation technology. This interest led to his association with Robert Fulton whom he met in France. The marble mantel was added around the 1820s. The room was renovated in the Colonial Revival style in the 1920s and appears as it did c. 1930. Photo: New York State Office of Parks, Recreation, and Historic Preservation.

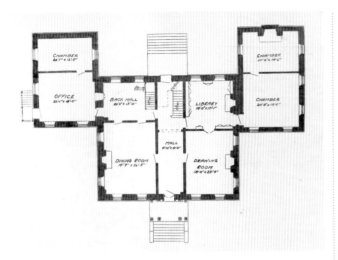

Speculative drawing of Clermont's floor plan. The original Clermont was a typical center hall plan structure, with four rooms on each floor. The north wing (left) was added in 1814; the south wing in 1831. New York State Office of Parks, Recreation, and Historic Preservation.

A reconstruction of Clermont as rebuilt in 1778 by Margaret Beekman Livingston, showing the early 19th-century wings. This unsigned drawing appeared in the second (1937) volume of *Great Georgian Houses of America*. Montgomery Place was also featured in this volume. Not surprisingly, Alice Delafield Clarkson Livingston of Clermont and General John Ross Delafield of Montgomery Place were among the subscribers.

The importance of the Livingston family reached its zenith in the career of the Chancellor—he held New York State's highest judicial post from 1777 to 1801. He was twice a delegate to the Continental Congress, participated in drafting the Declaration of Independence, served the new nation as its first Minister of Foreign Affairs (an office that became Secretary of State under the Constitution), and, as Chancellor, administered the first oath of office to George Washington. Bitterly disappointed when Washington refused to grant him a high cabinet post, and persuaded by Thomas Jefferson's political and philosophical views, Livingston helped establish the Jeffersonian Republican party in New York. Thomas Jefferson rewarded his efforts by appointing Livingston Minister to France in 1801. In 1803 Chancellor Livingston negotiated the Louisiana Purchase with Napoleon Bonaparte, but his clumsy attempt to take full credit for the deal led to his second fall from favor. This episode cost Livingston both a political future and due recognition in the history books for his critical role in the Purchase.

While in France, the Chancellor became associated with Robert Fulton (1765–1815), whose mechanical talents enabled Livingston to fulfill his long-held dream of building a practical steam boat. The Livingston-Fulton boat, christened the *North River* but commonly called *The Clermont*, made a successful maiden voyage between New York and Albany in 1807.

In 1793 Chancellor Livingston replaced Belvedere with a handsome, two-story, Neo-Classical style brick house. A greenhouse, or orangerie, built after Livingston's return from France, contained specimen fruit trees and exotic flora. A. J. Downing admired Clermont's pleasure grounds, citing the "level or gently undulating lawn, four or five miles in length, the rich native woods, and the long vistas of planted avenues."

Enslaved African-Americans and hired hands tended the Chancellor's house, gardens, and experimental farm. Tenant farmers worked several hundred small farms that Livingston owned on both sides of the river, which generated revenue for the Livingston family. But by the mid-19th century, growing resentment among many of the farmers resulted in the abolition of the tenant system, the Livingston family's economic power-base.

Old Clermont, as Margaret's house came to be called, gained a number of improvements, including the addition of the north wing (1814), a south wing (1831), and a third floor under a steeply pitched slate roof (1874 and 1893). John Henry Livingston (1848–1927) and his third wife and cousin, Alice Delafield Clarkson Livingston (1872–1964), redecorated the house in the mid-1920s in the Colonial Revival style, reflecting their concept of how the house appeared during the era of Chancellor Livingston. (The architects for these changes are not known.)

Complementing the house are well-documented gardens created by Alice Livingston between 1908 and the early 1930s meant to enhance surviving landscape and garden features of an earlier age. For example, she planted the hillside just east of the house with French hybrid lilacs to accent a "lilac walk" planted in the 1840s. The lilac walk connected "Old Clermont" and "New Clermont."

Clermont the seat of Mrs. Livingston 14 September 1796. Alexander Robertson, 1796. Pen and ink on paper, 9" x 11½". The house is shown as rebuilt by Margaret Beekman Livingston after the previous house was burned by the British during the Revolution. The artist indicates an open landscape surrounding the house, which fully exposes the spectacular views of the Hudson River and the Catskills. Today the setting of Clermont is more heavily wooded. From the collection of the McKinney Library, Albany Institute of History & Art.

New Clermont, located about 300 yards from the original house, deteriorated after Chancellor Livingston's death; it burned accidentally in 1909. Ruins of this important landmark house remain and have been stabilized by New York State. The house featured a central, two-story block flanked by four single-story wings. Julia Livingston Delafield, writing in 1877, reported, "Chancellor Livingston had chosen the capital letter H for the form of his house. The projecting wings in front were united by an elevated terrace, on which opened the windows of the dining-room on one side and of the drawing-room on the other, and which was filled with orange, lemon, and myrtle trees, not so common then as at present. A green-house ran the whole length of the house on the south side. In this green-house the dinner and supper tables were set on great occasions." Photo from Clarkson, 1869 (see bibliography).

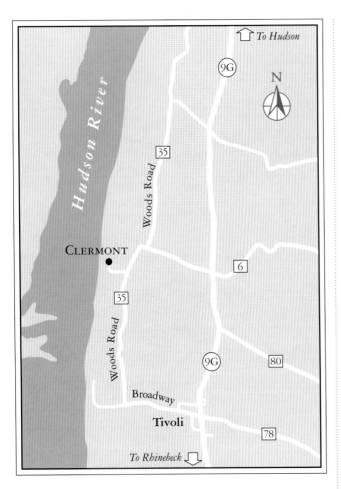

CLERMONT

A National Historic Landmark (1973)
New York State Office of Parks, Recreation, and
Historic Preservation.
One Clermont Ave.
Germantown, NY 12526
Telephone: 518/537-4240 or 518/537-TOUR.
Fax: 518/537-6240
Open April–October: Tuesday through Sunday and
Monday holidays. 11am–5pm; last tour at 4:30pm.
November–mid December: weekends, 11am–4pm.
*Museum Shop, visitor center, picnicking, historic trails,
special events, school programs, formal gardens. Grounds
available for weddings and private catering.*
Driving Directions: Entrance off Rt. 9G, 7.9 miles
north of the intersection of Rt. 9G and Rt. 199.
(This intersection is near the approach to the
Kingston-Rhinecliff Bridge.)

Clermont appears today much as it did in the late 1920s. Woodland trails and carriage roads, some dating to the 18th century, are still in use. Open fields north of the historic house attest to Clermont's agricultural heritage. The furnishings of the house, acquired during more than 200 years of Livingston habitation, are arranged as they were during the late 1920s by Alice Livingston and her two daughters who were living there. Among the portraits are works by John Wollaston, Gilbert Stuart, Thomas Sully, Rembrandt Peale, and William Sidney Mount.

In 1962, 90-year-old Alice Livingston transferred Clermont to the State of New York in a combination gift and sale, insuring its preservation. Her daughter, Honoria Alice Livingston McVitty, made subsequent gifts of property and possessions. Today, Clermont reflects in a tranquil and eclectic manner the continuity of seven generations of unbroken family ownership and that moment, frozen in time, when it came to a peaceful, public-spirited conclusion.

The Friends of Clermont, a not-for-profit membership organization, offers energetic support for the site's collections and programs.

MONTGOMERY PLACE

The lover of the expressive in nature, or the beautiful in art, will find here innumerable subjects for study. The natural scenery in many portions approaches the character of grandeur, and the foreground of rich woods and lawns, stretching out on all sides of the mountain, completes a home landscape of dignified and elegant seclusion, rarely surpassed in any country.

— ANDREW JACKSON DOWNING

Montgomery Place, a serene reflection of nearly 200 years of continuous family stewardship, is best known as an architectural landmark designed by Alexander Jackson Davis and a landscape influenced by the great Andrew Jackson Downing. But the *totality* of the estate—house, furnishings, gardens, woodlands, orchards, and hamlet—makes it a unique American treasure.

In 1775 General Richard Montgomery (1738–1775) was killed in the battle for Quebec and became the first hero of the American Revolution. His wife Janet Livingston Montgomery (1743–1828), at home on her place near Rhinebeck, became a revered widow, a status she cultivated for half a century.

In 1802, fifty-nine year old Mrs. Montgomery surprised her family by acquiring a working farm and building a new house she named "Château de Montgomery." She built

Entrance (east) front as designed by A.J. Davis. The splendid semi-circular portico with its composite capitals was added in 1863. Davis based his design on the Temple of Vesta, in Tivoli, not far from Rome. To the right is the arcaded north porch, which functioned as an outdoor room. Photo: Mick Hales (Historic Hudson Valley).

View of Montgomery Place, A.J. Davis, c. 1841, pencil on paper, 6¾ x 10. This view of the six-bay river (west) front of Montgomery Place shows Janet Livingston's Federal style house of 1805, and is the only surviving view of the house prior to its renovation by Davis. Collection of the Avery Library, Columbia University, A.J. Davis papers.

it to honor General Montgomery's memory and to provide a fitting legacy for his heirs; the French name derives in part from her brother Chancellor Livingston's tenure as Minister to France from 1801 to 1805. "She had ample pecuniary means," recalled Thomas Clarkson in 1869, "and good taste at command, the two needfuls in the successful improvement of a country estate."

At the terminus of a half mile-long allée of deciduous trees, some of which predated her arrival, Janet built a Federal-style house of stuccoed fieldstone. Here she developed a prosperous commercial enterprise of orchards, gardens, nursery, and greenhouse, tended by hired hands and enslaved Africans. Its beauty and marvelous westward vistas appealed to Janet, who noted charmingly, "Our eligant Mountains which bound the River so fantasticaly and varied, and our boasted Hudson which brings to its banks all we can desire is suficient to gratify any moderate American Woman."

General Montgomery's heirs, to whom Janet expected to leave Montgomery Place, predeceased her, and so Janet left the estate to her youngest brother, Edward Livingston (1764–1836). His fascinating lifetime of public service included terms as Mayor of New York City, United States Representative and United States Senator from Louisiana, and Secretary of State and Minister to France in the Andrew Jackson administration. Edward's cosmopolitan and well-traveled widow

Louise Livingston (1782–1860), a French-speaking native of Haiti, and their daughter Coralie Livingston Barton (1806–1873) used Montgomery Place as a summer home and remade its architecture and landscape over a forty-year period. They transformed the renamed Montgomery Place into a handsome, self-sufficient estate in the picturesque mode, adding a conservatory, intricate flower gardens, and architectural follies. Their comfortable lifestyle was supported by an ample domestic staff; the 1860 census reported three white and six free African-American house servants on the payroll.

For re-design of the house, Louise turned to the "taste, experience, & Skillful pencil" of A. J. Davis (1803–1892), the greatest American architect of the romantic movement. Adding porches, wings, balustrades, and other detail to Janet's original structure, Davis created a Classical Revival house in two phases, the first beginning in 1842 and the second during the early 1860s. Among the surviving features designed by Davis are the classical-style coach house, an Italianate farmhouse, and the unique Gothic Revival-style Swiss Cottage. A gatehouse, at least one folly in the conservatory garden, and a rustic Chinese bridge were among the unbuilt features proposed by Davis.

Andrew Jackson Downing (1815–1852), co-owner of

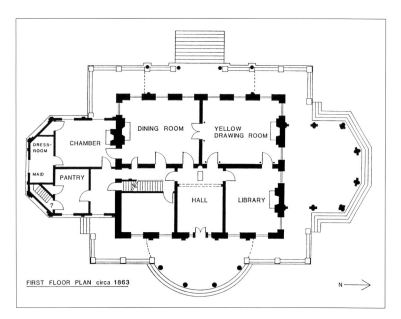

A. J. Davis did not modify Janet Montgomery's original interior plan (1805) but added porches to the north, west, and east, and a wing containing a series of small rooms to the south (left). Drawing from the Montgomery Place Historic Structures Report, 1988, Historic Hudson Valley.

A. J. Davis prepared this illustration of the north porch, published in A. J. Downing's *The Horticulturist* in the October, 1847 issue. Downing believed this to be the first outdoor living space in America.

a sophisticated nursery down river in Newburgh, advised informally on the gardens and grounds and on the layout of walks, statuary, rustic seats, and water features; sold the Bartons a variety of plants and trees; and, with Coralie Barton, designed the ornamental flower gardens surrounding the conservatory. Downing was the foremost American writer on landscape and garden subjects, editing the highly influential and nationally distributed monthly periodical *The Horticulturist;* he also wrote an important treatise on landscape design as well as architectural pattern books with architec-

tural drawings and illustrations by Davis. Not surprisingly, Downing wrote extensively about Montgomery Place, asserting that the estate "is second as it is to no seat in America, for its combination of attractions . . . all its varied mysteries of pleasure-grounds and lawns, wood and water."

Thomas Barton (1803–1869) began an arboretum in the 1840s, planning it with Hans Jacob Ehlers (c.1803–1858), a German landscape gardener. Writing in 1857, Henry Winthrop Sargent described Ehlers' design as "the most complete and satisfactory arboretum in the United States.... Neither pains nor expense have been spared in obtaining the most entire and thorough collection."

The post-Civil War period witnessed the decline of Montgomery Place, when it was occupied by relatives with life tenancy. Happily, the estate was inherited in 1921 by Livingston descendent General John Ross Delafield (1874–1964), a New York attorney, whose grandmother Julia Livingston Delafield had been a cousin and close friend of Cora Barton.

Gen. Delafield's energetic wife Violetta White Delafield (1875–1949), a talented botanist with a serious interest in horticulture, stabilized the rare, largely intact 19th-century landscape. She was responsible for the terraced landscaping on the west side of the house; a series of garden rooms for roses, herbs, and perennials; the romantic rough (or "wild") garden with its artificial stream and woodland plants; and the hedged ellipse with its pool for aquatics.

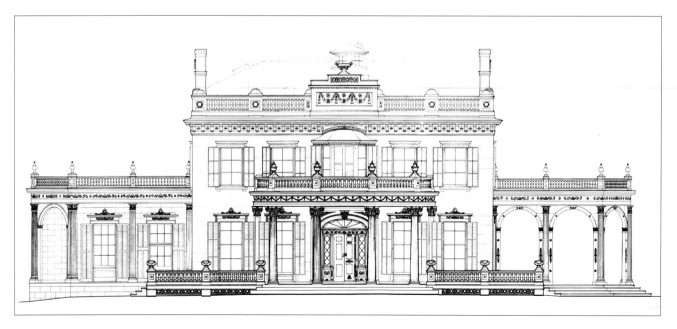

West elevation. The drawing highlights the carefully rendered, thorough program of classical ornament designed by A. J. Davis that enfolded the shell of Janet Livingston's Federal-style farmhouse. Drawing by Mendel, Mesick, Cohen, & Waite, Architects, Albany, NY, 1988, for Historic Hudson Valley.

View of the herb garden looking south toward the perennial borders. This quintessential Colonial Revival garden was created by Violetta White Delafield in 1939 on a site thought to have been the location of a 19th-century kitchen garden. A friend of Violetta's, Mrs. Ruthven A. Wodell, designed the garden, for which blueprints and planting plans survive. The garden contains over forty varieties of herbs, in beds defined by brick walkways laid in a serpentine pattern. The benches were reproduced in the 1980's from examples purchased by the Delafields for Montgomery Place in the 1920s and 1930s. Photo: Mick Hales (Historic Hudson Valley)

In 1839, the English artist and architect Frederick Catherwood (1799–1854) designed a Gothic Revival-style conservatory, which dominated the pleasure grounds. About 70 feet in length and filled with statuary, potted plants, urns, and furniture, it survived until about 1880. The "gardenesque" planting surrounding the conservatory was designed by A.J. Downing, working closely with Louise and Coralie Barton. Here is shown the rare *Agave americana*, or century plant, which Janet Livingston Montgomery is believed by family tradition to have received as a gift from her mother in the 1770s. The plant's bloom, which occurs only once in its lifetime, in 1873 was such a rare occurrence that the general public was invited—via newspaper advertising—to the grounds on certain days during the summer. Albumen print photograph, 1873, gift of J. Dennis Delafield, collection of Historic Hudson Valley.

Violetta White Delafield, circa 1915. Her daughter-in-law Margaret Delafield recalled, "She was a very volatile, electric person…. She loved gardens, she loved flowers, she loved plants. [Her own family] went to Italy almost every winter…and she became very aware of gardens—formal gardens, different kinds of gardens, the style of gardening. She was a very clever woman, and she became an expert in anything she was interested in." For example, she became a nationally recognized expert in *ikibana,* the art of Japanese flower arranging, which she took up, most remarkably, during World War II. Photo: collection of Historic Hudson Valley.

The Delafields added a hydroelectric generator, clay tennis court, squash court, and greenhouse, restored the 19th-century woodland walks, improved the orchards, and thoroughly renovated the house. General Delafield became an enthusiastic collector of furnishings and memorabilia with Livingston connections. Once again, Montgomery Place became a centerpiece of active and idyllic family life, with picnics and lawn parties, teas and dinners, tennis matches, swimming, boating, riding, and all the pleasures of privileged country living.

To ensure Montgomery Place's preservation, Delafield descendants conveyed title to Sleepy Hollow Restorations (now Historic Hudson Valley) in 1986. The combination of sale and gift included 434 acres of land, a portion of the hamlet of Annandale, orchards, gardens, and the house. Its contents were preserved, according to a family member, by "strong family tradition and the precept of saving and *never* throwing away." Letters and papers documenting the estate's

history were deposited in the Princeton and Historic Hudson Valley libraries. Historic Hudson Valley restored the house and grounds to a meticulous standard, opening the estate to the public in 1988.

MONTGOMERY PLACE

A National Historic Landmark (1992)
Historic Hudson Valley
River Road (PO Box 32)
Annandale-on-Hudson, NY 12504
Telephone: 914/758-5461
Fax: 914/758-0545
Internet: *www.hudsonvalley.org*
e-mail: *mail@hudsonvalley.org*
Open April–October, daily except Tuesdays. Open weekends from November to mid-December.
Museum shop, seasonal food service, picnicking, special events, school program. Available for weddings and private catering.
Driving directions: Entrance located off Rt. 9G approximately 2.9 miles north of the intersection of Rt. 9G and Rt. 199, near the approach to the Kingston-Rhinecliff Bridge.

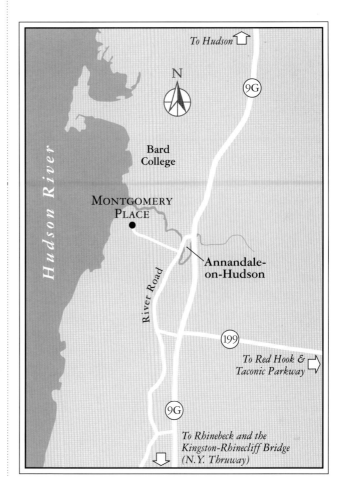

Entrance (east) front. A. J. Davis was responsible for the design of the Tuscan style villa, which envelopes the original late-Federal period farmhouse. The *porte-cochère*, octagonal extension, and tower were added by Davis. Photo: Richard Pileggi, 1997, for Historic Hudson Valley.

LOCUST GROVE
THE SAMUEL F. B. MORSE HOUSE * POUGHKEEPSIE

The mansion is so embowered that it is almost invisible to the traveller on the highway. But immediately around it are gardens, conservatories, and a pleasant lawn, basking in the sunshine, and through vistas between magnificent trees, glimpses may be caught of the Hudson, the northern and southern ranges of mountains and villages that dot the western shore of the river.

— BENSON LOSSING, 1866

Locust Grove is a Tuscan-style villa designed by Samuel Finley Breese Morse (1791–1872), the painter and inventor of the commercially viable telegraph, and by the eminent architect Alexander Jackson Davis (1803–1892). It was the Morse family home from 1847 until 1872. An eclectic combination of art, architecture, and landscape, Locust Grove reflects Morse's personal tastes as an artist and the trend-setting influence of Davis as a champion of new styles in architecture.

Henry Livingston (1714–1799), a grandson of the First Lord of Livingston Manor, purchased the property in 1751. His son Henry Livingston, Jr. (1748–1828) named it Locust Grove, farmed the land, and built a wharf and sawmill on the river. In 1830 John B. Montgomery (1785–1861) and his wife Isabella, a wealthy New York City couple (unrelated to Gen. Richard Montgomery of Montgomery Place), acquired the property as a "gentleman's estate" and built a late Federal-style house on the edge of the steep bluff, with striking river vistas to the north and south.

In 1847, the Montgomerys sold Locust Grove to Samuel F. B. Morse, a fifty-six year old widower seeking to unite his scattered family under one roof. With his arrival, Locust Grove entered a vibrant phase of expansion, development, and redesign. To his brother Sidney, Morse wrote excitedly,

I am almost afraid to tell you of its beauties and advantages. It is just such a place as in England could not be purchased for double the number of pounds sterling. Its 'capabilities,' as the landscape gardeners would say, are unequalled. There is every variety of surface, plain, hill, dale, glen, running stream and fine forest, and every variety of distant prospect; the Fishkill Mountains towards the south and the Catskills towards the north; the Hudson with its varieties of river craft, steamboats of all kinds, sloops, etc. constantly showing a varied scene.

Educated at Yale College and trained as an artist at the Royal Academy in London, Morse spent his early life as a portrait painter. He received several important com-

This view of a gothic villa in the country, a wood engraving after a postcard-sized oil painting by Morse, appeared as the frontispiece for Davis' book *Rural Residences*, 1837. Historic Hudson Valley library.

missions but never gained the prominence he hoped to achieve. While major canvases on historical themes failed to bring him financial success, his place in history as an artist was secured in 1825 when he formed and directed the National Academy of Design. The electromagnetic telegraph, perfected by Morse and successfully tested in 1844, was adopted across the country and around the world. Together with the invention of the Morse code, the telegraph completely revolutionized communications and finally brought Morse financial security. So it was science rather than art that enabled Morse to purchase Locust Grove.

In 1848, Morse married a cousin, Sarah Elizabeth Griswold (1822–1901), coincidentally a great-granddaughter of Henry Livingston, Jr., and began an ambitious building program at Locust Grove. Morse made numerous sketches of the existing building and his ideas for improvements. He consulted with his close friend, A. J. Davis, and together they drafted plans for the new house, completed in 1852. The best-known proponent of the romantic movement in the United States, Davis had published *Rural Residences* (1837) that explained his concepts for landscape and architectural design. A wood engraving of a small land-

West Lawn (c. 1871), with the elderly Samuel F.B. Morse in his wheelchair in the company of family members. The four-story Tuscan tower faces the Hudson River. The centerpiece of the Morse-Davis design, the tower contains the drawing room and family bedrooms above. A conservatory for the display of exotic plants, removed in the late 19th century, is visible at left. Collection of Locust Grove.

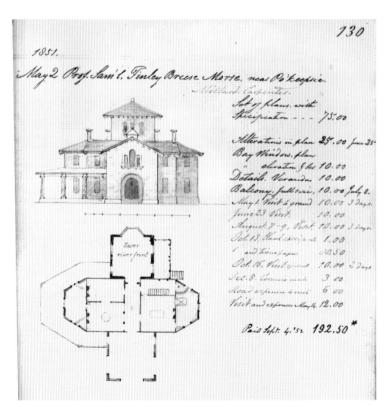

Detail of an invoice submitted by A.J. Davis to Samuel F.B. Morse (c. 1852) showing entrance facade and floor plan of Locust Grove. The invoice covered plans, specifications, architectural details, and site visits. The Metropolitan Museum of Art, Harris Brisbane Dick Fund, 1924 (24.66.1400).

scape painted by Morse in 1836 appeared as the frontispiece of the book.

With his artist's eye, Morse combined at Locust Grove lawns and colorful flower gardens that led the eye to the sparkling Hudson River. The great sweep of landscape from the house to the river—now in the beginning stages of restoration—was designed as a picturesque park, with clumps of trees, stone walls, water courses, and other landscape features.

At Locust Grove, Davis adapted a Federal-style house—just as he did at Montgomery Place—by giving it a new exterior treatment and polygonal extensions. For Locust Grove, Davis

View looking westward from the west lawn of the villa toward the Hudson River. (The river cannot be seen in the photo; the house in the distance is on the opposite side of the river.) Morse, certainly influenced by A. J. Davis and probably by A. J. Downing, used his knowledge of painting and landscape to create expansive park-like grounds between the house and the river, which incorporated lawns, trees, river views, and distant hills. Photo: Richard Pileggi, 1997, for Historic Hudson Valley.

and Morse designed a "Tuscan" style house, with an asymmetrical floor plan, simple ornament, and picturesque Italianate massing. To achieve the new plan, Morse expanded and altered the existing house in every direction, constructing wings to create an octagonal central block. On the east side, Davis added a *porte cochère*, and to the west a Tuscan tower, painted, sanded, and scored to suggest ashlar masonry, a technique he also used at Montgomery Place. This additional space accommodated Morse's expanding family, including three children from his first marriage and four children from his second.

Morse formed a close connection with the Poughkeepsie community, serving as a founding trustee of Vassar College. On a regional and national level, Morse remained involved in the continuing development of telegraphic communication, espoused a highly controversial political agenda, and was involved in extensive, high-profile litigation over his claim to having invented the telegraph. (His patent rights were established by a decision of the Supreme Court in 1854.)

Morse died in 1872, his wife, Sarah, in 1901. That year their heirs sold Locust Grove to William and Martha Young, who added a new dining room and bedrooms. William Young (1855–1909), a wealthy New York City lawyer, filled the house with eclectic collections of furniture, porcelain, and paintings and was active in Poughkeepsie society. The Youngs' daughter Annette Innis Young (1885–1975) lived at Locust Grove until her death.

Samuel F. B. Morse (seated in center) with his second wife Sarah (left), mother-in-law (far right) and other family members framed by the arch of the *porte cochère*. The photo (1860) demonstrates how Davis achieved a fresh new approach to the historical Tuscan style by editing and simplifying the details and massing of the traditional Roman arch. Collection of Locust Grove.

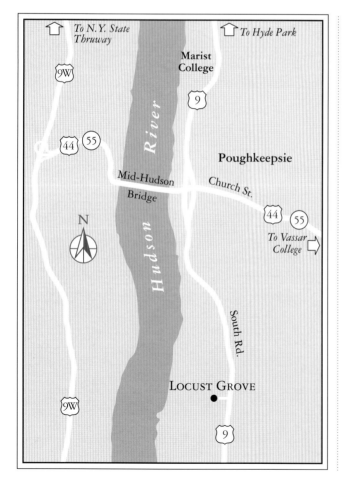

Well-known in the Poughkeepsie community for her support of numerous charitable causes, as well as her concern for preserving natural and historic resources, she provided a trust in her will to maintain her family's historic house and its 150 acres of gardens and woodlands for the "enlightenment, enjoyment, and visitation of the public."

LOCUST GROVE

A National Historic Landmark (1964)
370 South Road
PO Box 1649
Poughkeepsie, NY 12601-0649
Telephone: 914-454-4500
Fax: 914-485-7122
e-mail: *morse-historic-site@worldnet.att.net*
House open daily May through October. Otherwise, all tours by reservation. Grounds: Open year round, 8am to dusk, weather permitting.
Museum shop, picnicking, special events, school programs. Available for weddings and private catering.
Driving directions: Entrance located on Route 9 in Poughkeepsie, New York, 2 miles south of the Mid-Hudson Bridge (Route 44/55) or 11 miles north of I-84.

WILDERSTEIN

WILDERSTEIN PRESERVATION ✴ RHINEBECK

*It is strange to live in someone else's house—strange. . . —You always have your own home in the back of your consciousness.
The wind in the trees, even, is a strange wind, whereas there is an intimacy with the wind that sighs through the branches of the
pines outside my tower room at home—the creakings in the floor, the way the sun slants through the windows—no matter
how often you've heard them, they are strange compared to the creakings and sunlight at Home. . . .
Or is it simply a matter of where the heart happens to be? Most certainly, a large part of mine
lives permanently over there {at Wilderstein}. . . .*

— MARGARET SUCKLEY, 1936

High above the Hudson River, in an unspoiled setting, stands Wilderstein, an imposing late 19th-
century frame country house. The house,
grounds, and its fully intact contents—books, letters, photographs, paintings, and household objects of every kind—
document architectural and social history in the Hudson
River Valley. Now on the road to recovery from a state of
decay, Wilderstein demonstrates in the most evocative way
the fate of big, important houses owned by families whose
economic fortunes have declined but whose emotional
attachments to their ancestral home places have continued
unabated.

In 1888, Wilderstein was painted in a polychrome scheme. The original mauve, green, and Tuscan tan colors can be seen in the restored upper
portion of the tower. The brown paint dates from 1910, when the house was repainted entirely in that color; by that time, monochrome styles
had returned to favor. (The 1888 colors are being slowly restored.) Photo: Richard Pileggi, 1997, for Historic Hudson Valley.

In 1852 Thomas Holy Suckley (1810–1888) and his wife and cousin Catherine Murray Bowne Suckley (1823–1879) purchased 32 acres belonging to Wildercliff, an estate owned by a distant cousin and niece of Chancellor Livingston. The Suckleys were attracted by the varied terrain, picturesque views of the river, and, undoubtedly, the Livingston family associations.

Thomas was descended from both Robert Livingston (1654–1728), First Lord of the Manor, and Henry Beekman (1652–1716), patentee of Rhinebeck. Suckley's fortune had been secured through real estate investments and his father's export and banking business in New York. The Suckleys hired New York architect John Warren Ritch (born 1822), who gave them a two-story Italianate house closely resembling designs in his pattern book, *The American Architect* (1847–49).

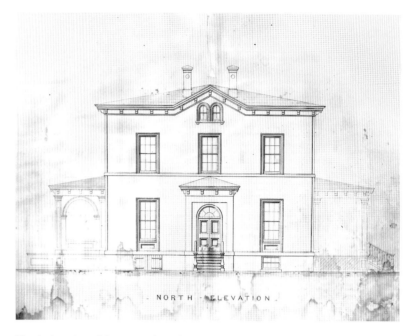

North elevation of the original, modest Italianate villa designed in 1852 by John Warren Ritch. Collection of Wilderstein Preservation.

Their only surviving child, Robert Bowne Suckley (1856–1921), inherited the estate in 1888. Trained as a lawyer, he lived on his inheritance, describing his occupation as "gentleman." He and his wife and distant cousin Elizabeth Philips Montgomery (1864–1953), also a Livingston descendant, extensively remodeled and enlarged the house. Poughkeepsie architect Arnout Cannon, Jr. (1839–1898) added a third story, *porte cochère*, wrap-around verandah, five-story tower, and servants wing. With electric lighting, anti-burglary systems, the architect's patented dumbwaiter, and polychrome exterior, Wilderstein represented the height of late-Victorian technology and fashion.

New York decorator Joseph Burr Tiffany (1856–1917), a cousin of Louis Comfort Tiffany, selected the stained glass windows, mantelpieces, and wall coverings. The windows of the mahogany-paneled dining room

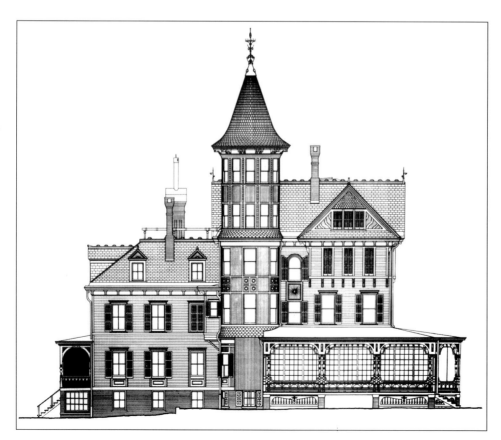

West facade. Wilderstein's irregular massing, tower, porches, and applied detail characterize it as Queen Anne in style. The verticality of the house as redesigned by Cannon was strongly emphasized by the five-story tower. Drawing by Steven Parsons for the Historic American Buildings Survey, National Park Service, 1975.

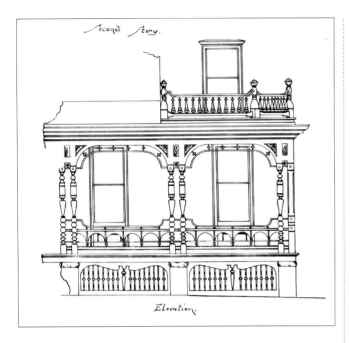

Arnout Cannon's drawing (1888–89) of the porch detail highlights the heavy, turned posts and spindled detail which served almost as picture frames for the splendid river views planned by Vaux. Collection of Wilderstein Preservation.

Cannon completely reconfigured the plan of the mid-19th-century villa, adding the servants wing (right), the broad wrap-around porch, and the *porte cochère*. A conservatory opening off the L-shaped dining room (top, center) was planned but not built. Drawing by Robert Anders for the Historic American Buildings Survey, National Park Service, 1975.

feature the crests of the Tillotson, Lynch, Chew, and Livingston families, and the newly-devised Suckley crest. The ground floor rooms, including the splendid oak-paneled stair hall, cozy Gothic detailed library, formal Louis XVI salon, and comfortable Colonial Revival parlor, offer a unique sampling of the eclectic decorative fashion during this period of American design.

Records from 1890 and 1891 indicate a staff of eight to ten house servants including a butler, cook, nurse, laundress, chamber maids, and waitresses. Twelve men worked on the grounds and farm.

In 1890, Suckley hired Calvert Vaux (1824–1895), one of the nation's premier architects and landscape designers, then in the twilight of his career, to improve the grounds. Vaux, architect of many houses in the Hudson Valley and Frederic Church's advisor at Olana, designed a network of trails and roads connecting buildings and traversing the sloping bluff to the river. Like the house, the landscape was oriented toward the Hudson; a path leads to points of interest and views of the marshy cove, river scenes, and distant hills. At low tide, one might spot "wild man's rock," the Indian petroglyph from which Wilderstein derives its mock-German name. Calvert Vaux, working with his son Downing Vaux, provided a planting plan which framed the extraordinary river views and the vistas from the lawns and spacious porches of the house. Downing Vaux also designed a cottage at Wilderstein which survives.

Following financial reversals in the 1890s, the Suckleys moved with their six children to Switzerland for a ten-year period. After Robert Suckley's death, his survivors struggled along, with their shrinking fortune further depleted by bad investments and the effects of the Depression. The eldest daughter, Margaret Lynch Suckley (1891–1991), became a companion to a neighboring aunt. Her modest salary supplemented her family's dwindling investment income, helping to cover the most pressing expenses of the estate and to support her mother, two brothers, and other family members.

In the 1920s, Miss Suckley (known as "Daisy") renewed her childhood acquaintance with her sixth cousin Franklin D. Roosevelt. (Daisy was actually more closely related to FDR's wife, Eleanor, through her Livingston

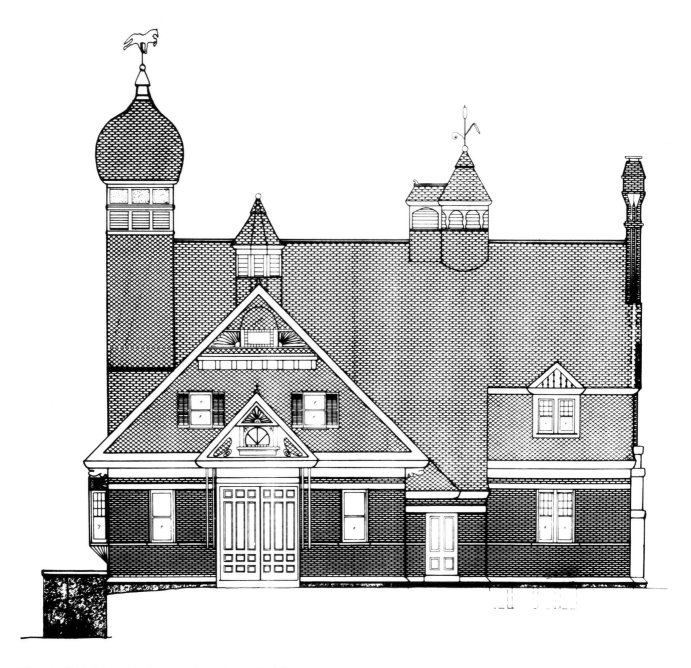

The splendid brick carriage house, with its slate roof and distinctive, onion-domed tower, was also designed by Arnout Cannon. Drawing by Elise M. Barry for Wilderstein Preservation, 1983. Other structures on the grounds included a Lord & Burnham greenhouse, a gate-lodge by Vaux (heavily altered), and a boat-house by Cannon (destroyed).

connections than she was to FDR through the Beekmans.) Their acquaintance evolved into a close and extensively documented friendship. FDR often addressed his letters to "MM" (My Margaret); Daisy often signed hers "YM" (Your Margaret). She played an important and discreet role as confidante and comforter to the President, recording his views on many issues, from New Deal projects to foreign policy, and observing him as an intimate friend and human being, rather than a political figure. Fala, FDR's beloved

Two Suckley brothers (at far right) and a number of their cousins pose formally at the entrance of Wilderstein in 1889 or 1890, about the time the new house was finished. Photo: Wilderstein Preservation.

Seated in rustic, Adirondack-style lawn chairs while watching a game of tennis at Wilderstein circa 1915 are (left to right) Robert B. Suckley, who inherited the place in 1888, his daughter Margaret ("Daisy") Suckley, his daughter Katharine, his niece Margaret Montgomery, and Katharine's twin sister Elizabeth. Photo: Wilderstein Preservation.

WILDERSTEIN

Wilderstein Preservation
64 Morton Road (PO Box 383)
Rhinebeck, NY 12572
Telephone: 914/876-4818
Fax: 914/876-3336
Internet: *www.enjoyhv.com*
Open May 1–Oct. 31, from noon to 4pm.
Special events, school program, Museum Shop.
Available for weddings and private catering.

Driving directions: From the center of Rhinebeck village, follow Rt. 9, driving 0.5 mile south. Turn right onto Mill Road, proceeding 2.4 miles; turn right onto Morton Road, proceeding 0.3 mile to entrance.

Scottie and the most famous presidential dog, was her gift to him.

In 1941 the President obtained for Daisy a job as a junior archivist at the newly built FDR Library at Springwood, which gave them convenient and frequent opportunities to enjoy each other's company. The intimacy of their friendship, kept secret throughout her long life, was unknown even to FDR's most recent biographers.

Daisy continued at the Library in Hyde Park until her retirement in 1963. In 1983, she gave her house and grounds to Wilderstein Preservation, a largely volunteer, not-for-profit corporation, retaining life tenancy. In 1991 she died where she had been born, at Wilderstein, just short of her 100th birthday. Daisy's diaries and the letters which she and Roosevelt exchanged were annotated and published by historian Geoffrey C. Ward in his book *Closest Companion* (1995). A number of letters have been sold to raise funds to preserve the estate; as a consequence, the restoration of Wilderstein progresses. The property not only presents distinctive architecture and landscape, but also reminds us of a profoundly touching "old-fashioned love story, genteel and clandestine," as Ward described it, between Daisy Suckley of Wilderstein and Franklin D. Roosevelt of Springwood.

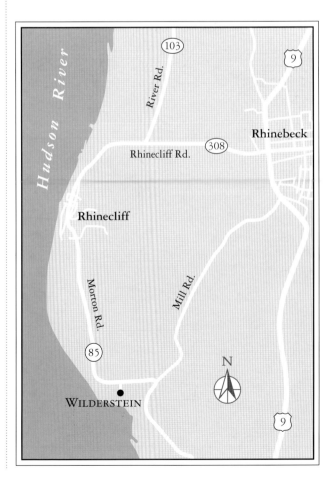

OLANA

I am building a house and am principally my own Architect.
I give directions all day and draw plans and working drawings all night.

— FREDERIC EDWIN CHURCH

Olana was the home and studio of the Hudson River School artist Frederic Edwin Church (1826–1900), among the most important painters in American history. He developed the estate as a three-dimensional work of art—a totally integrated environment embracing architecture, art, and landscape unmatched by any other 19th-century American property.

Church came from a prominent family in Hartford, Connecticut. His artistic ability and connections recommended him to Thomas Cole (1801–1848), considered the founder of the Hudson River School of painting. As Cole's student from 1844 to 1846, Church sketched and painted scenes in the Hudson Valley, including the panoramic view near the place that became Olana. Church's reputation grew as he traveled, sketched, and exhibited his paintings dramatizing the variety and splendor of North and South America. He rose to international prominence in 1857 with *Niagara*, an extraordinarily dramatic painting. At the New York City exhibition for his painting *Heart of the Andes* (1859) he met the beautiful Isabel Mortimer Carnes (1836–1899), whom he married in 1860. To secure privacy in which to raise his family and to paint, Church purchased a hard-scrabble farm distinguished by one of the most spectacular of all Hudson River views.

Church at first concentrated on transforming Olana into an ornamental farm. Like his contemporaries, Church recognized landscape gardening as a fine art, creating and composing real views and vistas as he did so imaginatively on canvas. Church laid out miles of roads, planted thousands of trees, dredged a marsh to create a ten-acre reflecting lake, and hired the youthful Richard Morris Hunt (1827–1895) to design a small, plain year-round house called "Cosy Cottage."

Two children born to the Churches in the early 1860s died of diphtheria in 1865. The next year, the grieving couple and their infant son, Frederic, Jr., began a series of extensive travels that eventually took them to England, where Church was exposed to the artists and architects of the Aesthetic Movement. They then traveled to the Middle East, acquiring hundreds of exotic objects. The desert landscapes and ancient cities moved Church profoundly and proved to be a transforming intellectual experience. He wrote that the "barren mountains and parched valleys possess the magic key that unlocks our innermost heart." This landscape was later the source of a series of paintings recording the history of human civilization.

On their return, the Churches discarded the elaborate designs for a large Châteauesque-style house prepared by Hunt. Their trip had radically changed their image of what a house should be. The Moorish architecture provided

OPPOSITE: Olana's dramatic south facing front. The main house and tower overlook the landscaped park and the river. The visual interplay of recessed porches, projecting balconies, soaring towers, and obliquely-angled awnings forms a powerfully dramatic composition. The artist's studio, added in 1888–91, extends to the left. Photo: Peter Aaron/Esto.

RIGHT: *Study of a House for F. E. Church, Esq., at Hudson, N.Y.,* Calvert Vaux, c. 1870. After consultation with Church, Vaux prepared this second perspective view of the proposed house. Collection of New York State Office of Parks, Recreation and Historic Preservation, Olana State Historic Site.

Court Hall, used by the family as a living room, was inspired by courtyards typical of domestic buildings of the Middle East. Church mixed the colors for the room on his palette, designed the stenciled wall ornament, and collected the exotic objects in the room. Photo: © 1996 Kurt Dolner.

Plan of the first floor. The original floor plan is simple and balanced: the cruciform Court Hall features large rooms between the arms of the cross and small rooms at the terminus of each arm. The studio addition of 1891 projects westward. The room labeled "Ombra" is a recessed porch. Collection of New York State Office of Parks, Recreation and Historic Preservation, Olana State Historic Site.

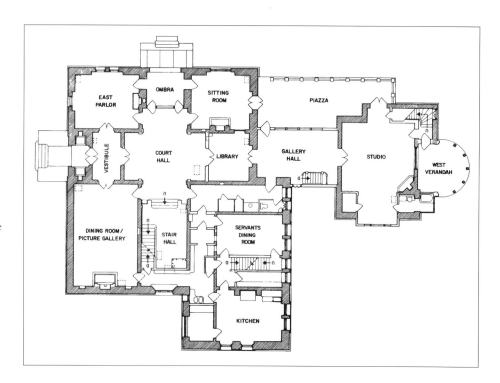

The Hudson Valley in Winter from Olana, Frederic Edwin Church, c. 1871–72. Oil on paper mounted on canvas, 20.25 x 13 inches. Church found the view from his studio "most beautiful and wonderful." Collection of New York State Office of Parks, Recreation and Historic Preservation, Olana State Historic Site.

a sense of permanence, rich associations with the Muslim and Christian past, and splendid decorative possibilities; the Aesthetic Movement stimulated their desire to design their home as a total work of art.

For reasons not entirely clear, the Churches replaced Hunt with Calvert Vaux (1824–1895). Recent scholarship indicates that Church was the designer, with Vaux providing crucial technical support and advice. Construction began in 1870, with the second floor habitable in late 1872. The sumptuously decorated first-floor rooms required several more years to complete. Church mixed the colors for every room and designed the exterior and interior stencil ornament. His attention extended to the placement of furniture, decorative objects, and paintings. "The whole house," commented a journalist in the middle 1880s, "is a museum of fine arts, rich in bronzes, paintings, sculptures, and antique and artistic specimens from all over the world." Another writer exclaimed, "One feels as if transported

LEFT: Front entrance to Olana, unknown photographer, circa 1890. The Middle Eastern arched entrance shelters two children who are almost certainly the grandchildren of William Henry Osborn, a lifelong friend and patron of artist Frederic Edwin Church. Both Isabel and Frederic Church died in Osborn's house on Park Avenue in New York City, in 1899 and 1900 respectively. The Islamic pattern encaustic tiles which surround the entrance front are of German manufacture. Photo: Olana State Historic Site, New York State Office of Parks, Recreation, and Historic Preservation.

into the Orient when surrounded by so much Eastern magnificence." Research suggests the name Olana comes from the word *Olane*, a fortress-treasure house in Persia.

During the late 19th-century, the public's taste for Church's romantic realism in painting waned as the Barbizon school grew in popularity, and Church was increasingly afflicted with arthritis. Despite these setbacks, Church continued to paint, asserting his belief in himself as an artist by adding a studio (1888–1891).

Throughout this period Church continued to develop the grounds. Using native material and working in the Picturesque style, Church composed landscape scenes contrasting broad pastoral vistas with woodland intimacy, sundappled carriage roads with dark, enveloping forests, the blue distant mountains with the bright waters of the lake and river. Shifts in the light, atmosphere, and seasons caused frequent changes in these scenes. The artist wrote, "I can make more and better landscapes in this way than by tampering with canvas and paint in the studio."

By the late 1890s, Olana was complete as a work of art. Church had created a harmonious union of buildings, landscape and scenery, perhaps instinctively fulfilling landscape gardener Andrew Jackson Downing's conception of "a country residence. . .and its grounds, making such a composition as a landscape painter would choose for his pencil." By coming at the end of the Picturesque period in landscape architecture, and by distilling many of the elements developed in earlier Hudson Valley landscapes, the Olana landscape serves as the period's definitive summation.

Olana was preserved by Church's heirs through 1964, when plans were made to auction the property. Olana Preservation, Inc., formed by art historian David Huntington (1922–1990), purchased the 336-acre property in 1966 with the assistance of New York State; soon after, the State took title, opened the house and grounds to the public, and assured the future of one of the nation's unique and most romantic artistic treasures.

The Friends of Olana, Inc., was established in the early 1970s and has grown into an exceptionally effective not-for-profit membership organization promoting the care and public enjoyment of the site.

Felix Bonfils (attributed), Frederic Edwin Church and his son, Frederic Joseph Church, in Beirut, 1868. Collection of New York State Office of Parks, Recreation and Historic Preservation, Olana State Historic Site.

OLANA

A National Historic Landmark (1965)
New York State Office of Parks, Recreation, and Historic Preservation.
RD 2, Hudson, NY 12534
Telephone: 518/828-0135
Fax: 518/828-6742
Open April through October, Wednesday through Sunday, from 10am–4pm. (Visitor Center and Museum Shop open 9:30am–4:30pm.) Admission tickets are limited, so reservations by telephone are strongly suggested. Groups of 12 or more welcome Wednesday through Friday mornings; reservations are required for groups.
Museum shop, picnicking, historic carriage roads, special events, school programs.
Driving directions: Entrance located off Rt. 9G, one mile south of the Rip Van Winkle Bridge. Alternatively, Olana is located on Rt. 9G about 18 miles north of the intersection of Rt. 9G and Rt. 199, near the Kingston-Rhinecliff Bridge approach.

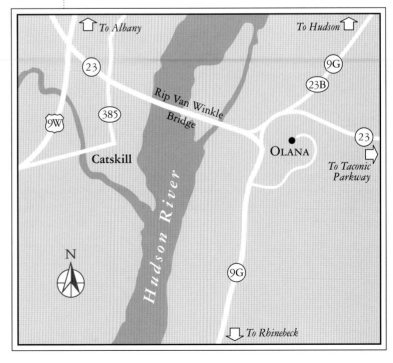

STAATSBURGH

MILLS MANSION STATE HISTORIC SITE AND
THE OGDEN AND RUTH LIVINGSTON MILLS MEMORIAL STATE PARK ✳ STAATSBURGH

The fragrance of the late blossoms seemed an emanation of the tranquil scene, a landscape tutored to the last degree of rural elegance.
In the foreground glowed the warm tints of the gardens. Beyond the lawn, with its pyramidal pale-gold maples and velvety firs,
sloped pastures dotted with cattle; and through a long glade the river widened like a lake under the silver light of September.

—EDITH WHARTON, FROM *The House of Mirth,* 1905

Staatsburgh evokes the theatrical grandeur of the Gilded Age, a period marked by the accumulation of great fortunes and accompanied by unprecedented spending on houses and lifestyles. Social critics contrast the conspicuous consumption of the *nouveaux riches,* such as the Vanderbilts of Hyde Park, with the conservatism of the region's old-money, landed gentry, like the Livingstons of Clermont. At Staatsburgh, however, one finds the aristocratic heritage of the Livingston family, long established and respected in the Hudson River Valley, infused with the new money of the Gilded Age.

Edith Wharton almost certainly used Staatsburgh as her model for Bellomont, a grand Hudson Valley estate in *The House of Mirth* (1905). In this best-selling novel of manners Edith Wharton provides a critical, behind-the-scenes look at the extended house-parties and competitive social positioning for which houses like this were built.

Gertrude Livingston (1757–1834) of Clermont, a great-granddaughter of the First Lord of the Manor, and her husband, General Morgan Lewis (1754–1844), acquired the site in 1792 and built a brick house there by 1795. Their granddaughter recalled it with

affection, writing that "it was as ugly as it was comfortable, but we children would have smiled at the absurdity of any one who ventured to say that it was surpassed in any particular by any establishment in America. . . ." When Livingston Manor, as it was then called, burned in 1832, it was replaced by a large Greek Revival-style house with Doric porticos. Lewis served at different times as Governor of New York, the state's Chief Justice, and Quartermaster General of the Army during both the Revolution and the War of 1812.

The Lewises' house passed to two successive generations and in 1890 was inherited by Ruth Livingston Mills (1855–1920), a great-great-great granddaughter of the First Lord of the Manor. Ruth had been married in 1882 to Ogden Mills (1856–1929), the son of Darius Ogden Mills (1825–1910). The father, a self-made businessman and banker, made his fortune in California after the discovery of gold in 1849, became well-established as an entrepreneur, investor, and philanthropist in New York City, and

OPPOSITE: Entrance (east) front. The house is constructed of load-bearing brick walls sheathed in stucco. The entablatures and moldings are run-in-place concrete; the applied details and the Ionic capitals are cast concrete. Photo: New York State Office of Parks, Recreation, and Historic Preservation.

RIGHT: The 50-foot-long Louis XIV-style dining room was added by White, together with an oak-paneled library of equal size. Régence-style chairs surround the mahogany table, expandable to seat 24. The cipollino marble walls are decorated by four 18th-century Flemish tapestries, likely acquired by Stanford White for the Millses. Photo: New York State Office of Parks, Recreation, and Historic Preservation.

left an estate of $60 million. Ruth's heritage and social status married to her husband's new money proved to be a winning combination in the Hudson Valley.

Ruth Mills became an ambitious society hostess in New York. In 1894 she and Ogden hired architect Stanford White (1853–1906) to redesign and enlarge her house. By 1896, the *New York Times* was able to report that "for a year past Mr. Ogden Mills has had a hundred men employed building for him on his country place at Staatsburg a home which, in furnishings and appointments will equal any mansion in New York City." Shortly thereafter, their friends the Frederick Vanderbilts began their house down the road, designed by White's partner Charles McKim.

White designed the immense stuccoed mansion to resemble an English country house of the late 18th century, incorporating in the center of the plan much of the Greek Revival house he found on the site, and adding two large wings and a monumental Ionic portico on the entrance front.

The interiors were decorated in a range of Beaux-Arts styles incorporating generous portions of gilt, marble, and oak paneling, all designed to create an environment of *luxe.* Proving the family's Hudson Valley social credentials was a collection of Livingston family portraits. Today the house

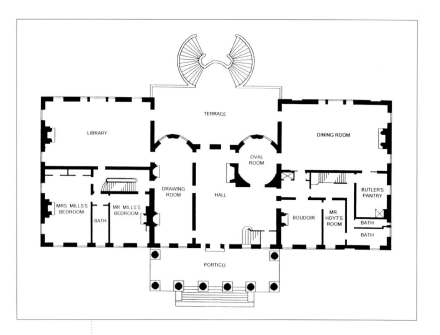

Main floor of the house as redesigned by Stanford White, who incorporated the center-hall plan Greek Revival house, less the wings, in the center section. The second floor contains 14 bedrooms for family and guests. Female servants lived in 10 bedrooms on the third floor; bachelor guests and male servants boarded in the basement, where there was also a billiards room. New York State Office of Parks, Recreation, and Historic Preservation.

is little altered and remains almost entirely as it was created for Ruth and Ogden Mills a century ago.

The grounds recall the English landscape style of the 18th century, with rolling lawns, informal plantings, and views carefully framed by ordered groupings of trees.

Unlike most estates in the region, the railroad at Staatsburgh runs well to the east of the house, which permits the landscaped grounds to roll uninterrupted to the banks of the Hudson. Typical of estates of the place and period, there were extensive special-purpose glass houses for growing ornamental plants for cutting and display, as well as vegetables and fruit for the table.

The handsome grounds were well suited for outdoor recreation, with riding and hiking paths, carriage trails, a boathouse and facilities for yachts, two tennis courts, and, on the edge of the property, a nine-hole golf course which the Millses shared with other families. In the winter when the river was frozen over, there was skating and ice-boating.

As at the nearby Vanderbilt estate, entertaining was seasonal. The Millses, who owned houses in New York City, Newport, Paris, and San Mateo County, California,

Entrance (east) front of the house, new in 1833, prior to its enlargement and remodeling by Stanford White. An identical tetrastyle portico sheltered the west front overlooking the river. "The plan," recalled Julia Livingston Delafield in 1877, "was drawn by my mother, and the result was a really handsome country house, more convenient than the first." Photo: New York State Office of Parks, Recreation, and Historic Preservation.

Entrance hall circa 1903. Stanford White carved this two-story monumental space from the 1832 Greek Revival house. The oak-paneled hall was furnished with a mix of English and French antiques and reproductions, which was a typical decorating practice. The potted palms and clipped bay trees were part of most fashionable Edwardian interiors. Photo: New York Office of Parks, Recreation, and Historic Preservation.

used Staatsburgh from September to January. About 24 servants kept the household running. The staff typically included an English butler and footmen, a retinue of Irish maids, a French lady's maid for Mrs. Mills, a French chef, and German or Swedish governesses.

The Millses' twin daughters married "successfully." The wedding of Gladys (1883–1970) in 1907 to Henry Carnegie Phipps (1879–1953) was lavish and widely publicized. Beatrice (1883–1972) married the 8th Earl of Granard (1874–1948), an Irish peer, fulfilling the Gilded Age society matron's dream of marrying her daughters to titled Europeans.

The Millses' son, Ogden Livingston Mills (1884–1937), inherited the estate in 1929. A lawyer by training, he participated in New York State politics, served three

Portrait of Ruth Livingston Mills, painted by Francois Glamony, 1909. Oil on canvas, 45" x 58". The portrait hangs in Mrs. Mills' sitting room.

41

Two ranges of glass houses were built between 1903 and 1910 to the south side of the house. Roses, gardenias, and orchids supplied Staatsburgh and the Mills house in New York. The most recent structure, the 1910 rose house (center), was manufactured by Lord & Burnham. The glass structures were removed in the late 1940s. Photo circa 1910. New York State Office of Parks, Recreation, and Historic Preservation.

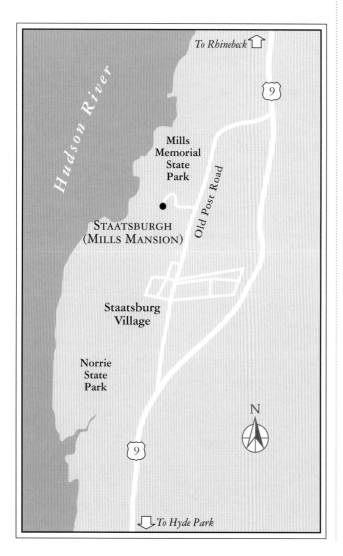

terms in Congress, and succeeded Andrew Mellon as Treasury Secretary in the Herbert Hoover administration. When Hoover lost the 1932 election to Mills' Hyde Park neighbor Franklin Roosevelt, Mills' career in public office ended; however, Mills continued as a leading national spokesmen for the Republican Party.

The estate passed to his sister Gladys Mills Phipps who gave it to the State of New York as a memorial to her parents, adding the contents of the house to her gift in 1970. At that time the formal name of the house was changed to Mills Mansion, although historically it had been known as Staatsburgh. The Friends of Mills Mansion, established in 1988, support New York State's preservation and public education programs.

Staatsburgh

New York State Office of Parks, Recreation, and Historic Preservation.
PO Box 308, Staatsburg, NY 12580
Telephone: 914/889-8851
Fax: 914/889-8321
Open April–Labor Day, Wednesday–Saturday: 10am–5pm; Sunday 12–5pm. Labor Day–October, Wednesday–Sunday 12–5pm. Special Christmas hours. Please call for other times.
Museum shop, picnicking, special events, school program.
Driving directions from the north (Rhinebeck): Follow Rt. 9, going south 4.6 miles from the center of the village of Rhinebeck to Old Post Road. Take Old Post Road 0.9 miles to the estate entrance.
Driving directions from the south (village of Hyde Park): Follow Rt. 9 going north 3.3 miles beyond the entrance to Hyde Park (Vanderbilt estate). Take Old Post Road 1.3 miles to the estate entrance.

LANDMARKS IN THE TOWN OF HYDE PARK

A trip to the town of Hyde Park offers the visitor an opportunity to visit four landmark properties managed by the National Park Service: Hyde Park, known more familiarly as the Vanderbilt mansion; Springwood, the family home of Franklin D. Roosevelt; Val-Kill, the retreat of Eleanor Roosevelt; and the FDR Library and Museum.

The "Hyde Patent" was issued in 1704 by the Governor of the province of New York, the notoriously corrupt Edmund Hyde, Viscount Cornbury, to four partners, who named the *estate* Hyde Park in his honor. The neighboring settlement was established as Stoutenburgh about forty years later, and by the early 19th century the settlement and the surrounding township had both taken the name Hyde Park. By that time, the estate had become known for its house and distinctive landscaped grounds.

The Hyde Patent comprises, roughly, the northern part of the present town. The southern part of the town occupies part of what was known as the Great Nine Partners Patent of 1697. Access to the waterfront was divided into nine shares. The Roosevelt family's present-day Springwood stands on what was originally known as Water Lot Number 6.

This map serves as a locator for all four places in the Town of Hyde Park which are described in the remaining pages of this guidebook.

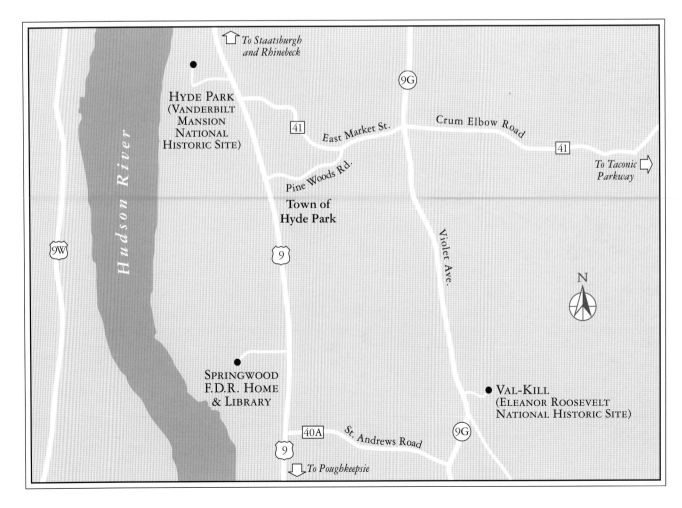

HYDE PARK

Hyde Park, on the Hudson, formerly the seat of the late Dr. Hosack, now of W. Langdon, Esq., has been justly celebrated as one of the finest specimens of the modern style of Landscape Gardening in America. Nature has, indeed, done much for this place, as the grounds are finely varied, beautifully watered by a lively stream, and the views are inexpressibly striking from the neighborhood of the house itself, including, as they do, the noble Hudson for sixty miles in its course. . . . Large and costly hot-houses were erected by Dr. Hosack, with also entrance lodges at two points on the estate, a fine bridge over the stream, and numerous pavilions and seats commanding extensive prospects; in short, nothing was spared to render this a complete residence.

— ANDREW JACKSON DOWNING

Hyde Park, a spectacular Gilded Age estate, documents the immense economic, social, and artistic changes America experienced after the Civil War, and in particular the Vanderbilt family's own economic and social achievement. However, fifty years before the Vanderbilts arrived, Hyde Park's romantic landscape had already earned it great distinction.

David Hosack (1769–1835), a physician, botanist, amateur horticulturalist, founder of the Manhattan's Elgin Botanical Gardens, and professor at Columbia College, acquired the property in 1829 from the estate of Samuel Bard. Bard, a physician and a founder of New York Hospital, was a pioneer in experimental horticulture and agriculture who had formed an impressive collection of plants and trees on the property.

Hosack built a handsome Greek Revival house and a glass house to go with it, established ornamental flower gardens, conducted horticultural experiments, and planted exotic specimen trees. Most importantly, he engaged André Parmentier (1780–1830), a landscape architect and plantsman who had emigrated from Belgium. In his seminal *Treatise*, A. J. Downing described Parmentier as one of the earliest professional landscape gardeners in America and "the only practitioner of the art, of any note." Parmentier's efforts, according to Downing, "effected, directly, far more for landscape gardening in America, than those of any other individual whatever."

OPPOSITE: The dining room was decorated by Stanford White around a ceiling the architect probably purchased in Europe prior to the design of the house. White also acquired the room's two fireplace surrounds and over-mantels, and the huge, 16th-century Isphahan rug on shopping expeditions to Italy, France, and England. The table, expandable to seat 30, and Louis XIV-style chairs were made in the late 19th century. Photo: Mick Hales, 1997, for Historic Hudson Valley.

William Stanley Haseltine (1835–1900). *Near Hyde Park, Hudson River.* July, 1860. Pencil and wash drawing on paper, 14⅝ x 21⅛ inches. M. and M. Karolik Collection. Courtesy, Museum of Fine Arts, Boston. This clearly rendered, park-like view looks northwest from a spot near Hyde Park; it captures the estate's extraordinary setting high above the floodplain and the breathtaking views of the valley and the Catskill Mountains in the distance. Haseltine was a Philadelphia native and artist who lived most of his life in Europe, mainly Italy.

Parmentier designed an expansive romantic landscape garden, one of the first in the nation. His sophisticated mix of tree groupings, panoramic vistas, temples, roads, and bridges immediately became a beacon for visitors. John Claudius Loudon (1793–1843), the pre-eminent British authority on the subject, noted Hyde Park as one of the finest American landscapes in his widely disseminated *Encyclopedia of Gardening* (1835). Downing wrote that Hyde Park was, for a period of time, "the finest seat in America."

In 1838, John Jacob Astor (1763–1848) acquired the estate for his daughter Dorothea and her husband Walter Langdon. For forty years, beginning in the early 1850s, Hyde Park was the country seat of their son Walter Lang-

TOP: The exceptionally handsome, Greek Revival style house was built circa 1847 by the Langdons to replace Dr. Hosack's house which had burned in 1845. Found to be structurally unsound, it was razed by the Vanderbilts but clearly influenced McKim's design for the new house. Photo circa 1895 courtesy National Park Service, Roosevelt-Vanderbilt National Historic Sites, Hyde Park, New York.

ABOVE: The White Bridge, an extraordinarily elegant single span structure carrying the entrance drive over Crum Elbow Creek, was designed by W. T. Hiscox & Co. of New York City and built in 1897. It is believed to be the first steel and concrete bridge in the nation. Photo circa 1898: FDR Library, Hyde Park.

RIGHT: An approximation of the formal garden terraces as they are believed to have appeared in 1938, the year Frederick Vanderbilt died. The left half of the plan shows architect James Leal Greenleaf's new designs for the Vanderbilts; the right half was established in the 1870s prior to the Vanderbilt era, though modified extensively by Greenleaf and others through the mid-1930s. The glass houses shown in the drawing replaced similar 19th-century structures erected by the Langdons. Drawn by the National Park Service, 1965.

don, Jr., whose wife, née Catherine Livingston, was a great-great-great granddaughter of the First Lord of the Manor. In 1894, when the property came on the market, Ogden Mills brought his friends Frederick William Vanderbilt (1856–1938) and Louise Anthony Torrance Vanderbilt (1844–1926) to see it. The Vanderbilts added Hyde Park to their collection of houses in Newport, Bar Harbor, the Adirondacks, and New York. Like the Millses, they hired McKim, Mead, and White to work on the house.

The brilliant Charles Follen McKim (1847–1909) was the principal architect; Ogden Codman, Jr. (1863–1951), Stanford White (1853–1906), and Georges A. Glaenzer (1848–1915) decorated and furnished the house. McKim, Mead and White also designed several other structures, including the gate lodges and guest-house. A Queen Anne-style stable complex was designed in 1897 by Robert Henderson Robertson (1849–1919), who had designed the splendid Shelburne Farms estate in Vermont for Frederick's sister Lila Vanderbilt Webb.

Hyde Park complemented the houses built by Frederick's near manic house-building siblings (see chart.) Hyde Park, completed in 1898, was comparatively modest by Vanderbilt standards but provided a generous measure of gilded grandeur. The Vanderbilts used Hyde Park in the spring, fall, and occasionally at Christmas. As many as sixty-five employees, mostly hired from local farm families, maintained the estate and the Vanderbilt way of life.

In 1901 Frederick Vanderbilt hired Charles A. Platt (1861–1933), an architect early in his distinguished career,

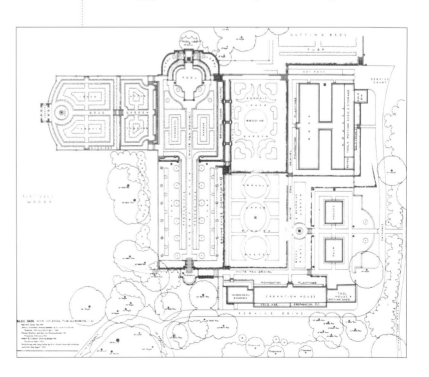

The Vanderbilt mansion is of steel frame construction, with brick in-fill and a veneer of Indiana limestone. Built, decorated, and furnished at a cost of about $3 million, the house is one of the two or three grandest country houses ever built by McKim, Mead, and White. Photo: Richard Pileggi, 1997, for Historic Hudson Valley.

to work on the landscape. However, for reasons unknown, the Vanderbilts replaced Platt with the aptly named landscape architect James Leal Greenleaf (1857–1933), who made substantial changes and improvements to the formal gardens, added a new set of glass houses (the third built on the estate), and preserved and nurtured the Parmentier landscape. Later changes to the formal gardens were provided by the prominent Philadelphia nursery and landscape firm of Thomas Meehan & Sons, by Robert Cridland, a landscape architect who had trained at the Meehan firm, and by Frederick Vanderbilt himself.

After Louise's death in 1926, Frederick, a shy, quiet man, enjoyed a simple social life with family and close friends, pursuing his interests in business, yachting, gar-

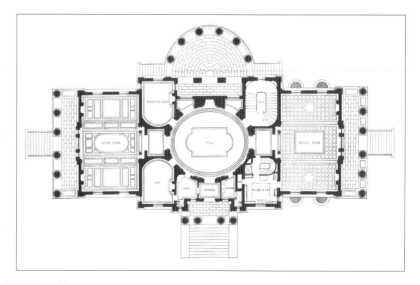

First floor plan for Hyde Park, reproduced from *A Monograph of the Work of McKim Mead & White 1879–1915*, published 1915–1920 in installments. The first floor plan featured an entrance hall and just four public rooms: two exceptionally large rooms for entertaining, and two smaller, more intimate spaces.

This small but beautiful building, constructed of limestone, is one of two designed by McKim, Mead, and White which functioned as gatehouses to the estate. Photo circa 1899: FDR Library, Hyde Park.

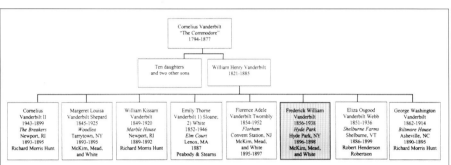

Every son and daughter of William Henry Vanderbilt (1821–1885) who reached maturity, eight in all, built splendid country houses, mostly in the 1890s. Hyde Park was the last to be finished. Frederick and his sisters Margaret and Florence commissioned McKim, Mead, and White. Frederick's three brothers commissioned the brilliant Richard Morris Hunt. (Note that the chart outlines most, though not all, of the country houses built by the family, and none of the spectacular city houses.)

dening, and gentleman-farming. He died in 1938, by which time his carefully managed fortune had grown to nearly $80 million, making him one of the richest men in America.

After inheritance taxes took half of Frederick Vanderbilt's estate, much went to educational institutions. The Vanderbilts had no children, and Margaret Louise (Daisy) Van Alen (1876–1968), a Newport socialite and a favorite niece, inherited Hyde Park and attempted unsuccessfully to sell it.

As it happened, Frederick Vanderbilt's death concluded Hyde Park's brief history as a private house. Few estates like these survived the imposition of the income tax, progressive inheritance taxes, and the Depression. And as the Depression deepened, the estate contributed to the impression that America had become a society of "haves" and "have nots," which helped to end the economic system in which such a house as this could comfortably exist. So like most houses of this scale and period, the Hyde Park of the Vanderbilts was enjoyed by only one generation.

President Franklin D. Roosevelt, Frederick Vanderbilt's Hyde Park neighbor, arranged for the acquisition of the property by the newly formed Historic Monuments Division of the National Park Service. Cited as a significant early 19th-century landscape populated by mature specimen trees as well as an intact document of the Gilded Age, the 212-acre property opened to the public in 1940. The first superintendent reported directly to President Roosevelt.

The immaculate gardens deteriorated after World War II. However, the National Park Service and the Frederick W. Vanderbilt Garden Association, Inc., a group of dedicated volunteers founded in 1984, have made significant progress toward their replanting and restoration.

HYDE PARK

A National Historic Site (1940)
National Park Service
Roosevelt-Vanderbilt National Historic Sites
Hyde Park, NY 12538
Telephone: 914/229-2414
Fax: 914/229-0739
e-mail: *ROVA_webmaster@nps.gov*
Internet: *www.nps.gov/VAMA*
Open daily year-round from 9am to 5pm.
Museum Shop, historic trails, special events.
Entrance on Rt. 9 in the village of Hyde Park.

Springwood

The Franklin D. Roosevelt National Historic Site ✳ Hyde Park

My husband always loved taking people he liked home with him.
I think he felt he knew them better once they had been to Hyde Park.

— Eleanor Roosevelt

S pringwood was the lifelong home of Franklin D. Roosevelt (1882–1945), four-term President of the United States, who led the nation out of the Great Depression and to victory in World War II. Throughout these momentous times, Roosevelt maintained his passion for his quiet Hudson River place, writing prior to his fourth presidential election, "All that is within me cries out to return to my home on the Hudson River." The site is the only presidential home where a President was born, grew up, married, raised his children, and was buried. Consequently it evokes authentic and deeply personal memories.

In 1867, James Roosevelt (1828–1900), an investor and wealthy landowner with deep roots in the Hudson River Valley, and Rebecca Howland Roosevelt, his first

Members of the Roosevelt family pose just outside Springwood's front door on September, 15, 1931. Sara Delano Roosevelt is seated next to her son, FDR, in the front row; Eleanor Roosevelt is standing behind her husband. Photo: FDR Library, Hyde Park.

The Georgian Colonial-style entrance facade as designed by Francis L.V. Hoppin. This new front provided an impressive and photogenic stage set for the ceremonial reception of visitors, occasional speeches, election night victory rallies, and other events. Photo: Richard Pileggi, 1977, for Historic Hudson Valley.

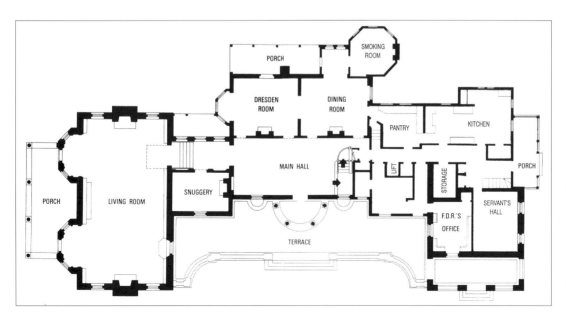

The center sections of the 19th-century villa were largely retained, and the flanking wings, entrance porch, terrace, and verandah were added in 1915. Courtesy National Park Service.

The oak-paneled family library, the largest room at Springwood, was added in 1915. There was no room anywhere more beloved by Sara and Franklin Roosevelt than this, which they jointly created. The portrait of Isaac Roosevelt (1726–1794) over the fireplace, one of two fireplaces in the room, is attributed to Gilbert Stuart. The Chinese porcelains came from the Delano family, whose fortune was made in the China trade. The plaster image of Winged Victory of Samothrace was a gift to Sara Roosevelt from the French government, in 1934, just after FDR began his first term as president. Sara took frequent European pleasure trips and regularly visited France. Photo: Mick Hales, 1997, for Historic Hudson Valley.

wife, purchased 110 acres and a rambling, Italianate-style frame house overlooking the Hudson River to replace their nearby house which had burned. The original Springwood, believed to have been built between 1800 and 1826, had been expanded over the years; the charming carpenter gothic gardener's cottage was added in the 1840s.

Four years after his wife's untimely death in 1876, James Roosevelt married Sara Delano (1854–1941), a well-connected woman half his age from Algonac, a large Hudson River house near Newburgh. (Interestingly, Algonac had been remodeled in the Italianate style by Downing and Vaux.) Their only child, Franklin Delano Roosevelt, was born in an upstairs bedroom at Springwood on January 30, 1882. James Roosevelt and his new wife continued mak-

ing improvements to the house and estate and added the large carriage barn in 1886.

At Springwood, young Roosevelt enjoyed a privileged but solitary boyhood among the unostentatious, old-money Hudson Valley aristocracy. Though the family spent winters in New York and summers on Campobello Island, in Canada, Springwood was the family seat. Here FDR developed his passion for the outdoors, spending his leisure time riding, ice-boating, fishing, and walking the woods and fields. When he was eight, his father became a semi-invalid, and the son was raised by his doting mother and tutored at home until he left for Groton, a boys' boarding school, and then Harvard College, class of 1904.

In 1905 he married a fifth cousin, Anna Eleanor

The Italianate, Hudson Valley bracketed villa was known as Brierstone prior to its purchase by the Roosevelts, who renamed it Springwood. It was this rambling frame house in which FDR was born and raised to adulthood; in 1915, when FDR was in his early thirties, it was transformed into a Georgian Colonial-style showplace. Photo: FDR Library, Hyde Park.

Roosevelt (1884–1962), a niece of President Theodore Roosevelt (1858–1919). Unlike her husband, Eleanor was connected to the Livingston family (she was a great-great-great granddaughter of Chancellor Robert Livingston) and had lived for 13 years with her Grandmother Hall, her guardian, at Oak Lawn (later called Oak Terrace), the Hall estate near Tivoli. The young couple lived in New York in a duplex town house designed by Charles A. Platt, which his mother built to share with them; they also lived with his mother at Hyde Park. Sara envisioned her son as the squire of Springwood, tending to the estate and participating in local affairs. But in 1910, at age 28, Franklin won election to the State Senate and began his path to the Governor's Mansion in Albany and to the White House.

In 1915 Sara and FDR enlarged Springwood to accommodate his growing family. FDR was then Under Secretary of the Navy, enjoying his promising and rapidly improving political status. Francis L.V. Hoppin (1866–1941), of the firm of Hoppin, Koen, & Huntington, drew up the plans. Hoppin was a socially well-connected New York architect and a Roosevelt family acquaintance who had been a leading draughtsman in the office of McKim,

Mead, and White before founding his own firm in 1894. At the time he began working for the Roosevelts his work included Rhinebeck's Church of the Messiah (1896), nearby Blithewood (Annandale-on-Hudson, 1901), The Mount for Edith Wharton (Lenox, MA, 1902), and the New York City Police Headquarters (1909). Hoppin's plans for the Roosevelts included wings to the north and south and a new, symmetrical Georgian Colonial-style facade of stucco and native fieldstone. Included in the renovations were a handsome new library, and a three-room suite for the young couple that later became three bedrooms—one each for Eleanor, Franklin, and Sara Roosevelt. Undoubtedly, FDR was closely involved in the redesign, making preliminary sketches and a detailed model. On the outside, Springwood boasted a grand, new presence, ably serving as a stage-set for FDR's political rallies and speeches. Inside, where the original rooms were little altered, Roosevelt installed his stamp collections, stuffed birds, ship models, and collections of naval prints. Sara, always critical of change and ostentation, called the 35-room house "our new hotel."

Sara owned and managed Springwood, with a staff of

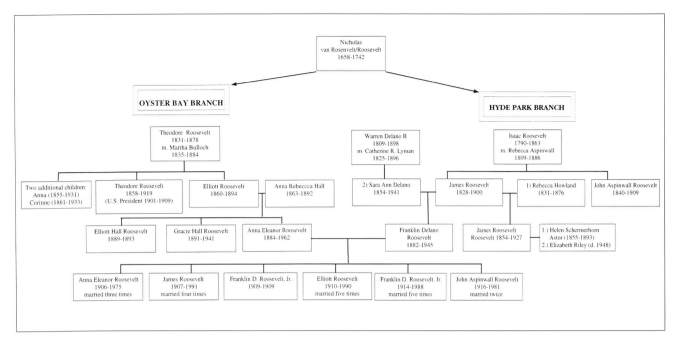

The chart shows selected members of the Roosevelt family tree, including Eleanor and Franklin Roosevelt's parents and children. FDR was a member of the "Hyde Park" branch of the family; Eleanor Roosevelt was a member of the "Oyster Bay" (Long Island) branch. Franklin and Eleanor Roosevelt's common ancestor was Nicholas Roosevelt (1658–1742), so their actual kinship was remote. (Theodore Roosevelt and FDR were fifth cousins; Eleanor was President Theodore Roosevelt's niece, making her FDR's fifth cousin once removed.) At the time of their wedding in 1905, Eleanor's uncle was President of the United States; their wedding in New York City was scheduled to permit the President to attend the wedding and escort Eleanor to the altar.

eight to ten house servants, later supplemented by domestic staff in the presidential entourage. The quintessential *grande dame*, Sara remained household head and hostess until her death, motivating Eleanor to remark that "for over forty years I was only a visitor there." FDR was nearly 60 when he inherited Springwood from his mother and out of respect for her memory made no changes.

Throughout FDR's career, Springwood was a political headquarters and refuge that he could return to in times of duress and strain brought on by domestic and international crises. During his 12-year presidency he made as many as 200 visits, mostly by rail from Washington. Springwood was also a place for entertaining special visitors, dignitaries, and heads of state, including Prime Minister Winston Churchill and Queen Wilhelmina of The Netherlands. Sara's greatest social triumph was the visit of Great Britain's King George VI and Queen Elizabeth in 1939.

In his will the President arranged for lifetime rights to Springwood for Eleanor and their children. After FDR's death, the family waived these rights and turned over the house, much of the contents, and some of the grounds to the National Park Service. Though Sara's fervent wish was that Springwood would remain the family seat, Roosevelt and his wife knew that the age of the ancestral Hudson

River estate occupied by families living on inherited wealth had been largely swept away by social, economic, and political change which, ironically, the Roosevelt administration had actively encouraged.

Eleanor was able to buy her own retreat, Val-Kill, from FDR's estate. Their son Elliott sold the remaining acres in parcels to developers, with the resulting effect on the once picturesque village clearly evident, and the community of Hyde Park became a popular tourist destination.

SPRINGWOOD

A National Historic Site (1944)
National Park Service
Roosevelt-Vanderbilt National Historic Sites
Hyde Park, NY 12538
Telephone: 914/229-2501
Fax: 914/229-0739
Open daily year round, from 9am to 5pm.
e-mail: *ROVA_webmaster@nps.gov*
Internet: *www.NPS.gov/HOFR*
Bookstore, historic trails, special events.
Entrance located on Rt. 9 in the village
of Hyde Park.

Val-Kill Cottage, originally the home of Val-Kill Industries, became Eleanor's home about 1936, when the factory ceased operation. Photo: Richard Pileggi, 1997, for Historic Hudson Valley.

VAL-KILL

ELEANOR ROOSEVELT NATIONAL HISTORIC SITE ✳ HYDE PARK

Val-Kill is where I used to find myself and grow. At Val-Kill I emerged as an individual.

—ELEANOR ROOSEVELT

Val-Kill was the private country retreat of Eleanor Roosevelt (1884–1962), the most influential and admired woman in American history.

Harry Truman described Eleanor Roosevelt as "First Lady of the World." As the wife of a disabled President, she was frequently "her husband's eyes and ears" and played an active, independent, and bona-fide partnership role. She had significant and unprecedented impact on national policy during FDR's long presidency, a critical period in the nation's history.

After her husband's death, Eleanor's popularity continued to grow, based upon her own accomplishments, and she functioned actively on the world stage. As a humanitarian and champion of liberal causes, particularly civil rights for black Americans, she became even more controversial than her husband and, as a consequence, was both beloved and detested. As a delegate to the United Nations during the Truman administration, she chaired the committee that drafted the Universal Declaration of Human Rights. She was a newspaper, radio, and television journalist, an author, peripatetic world traveler, unofficial American ambassador-at-large, riveting speaker, counselor to presidents, and head of a large family.

Val-Kill's architectural simplicity mirrors Eleanor's self-effacing personality and preference for plain living. It recalls the intensely emotional joys and tragedies she experienced in her private life. These included her difficult and lonely childhood; her discovery in 1918 of her husband's affair with Lucy Mercer, which nearly ended her marriage; her uneven relationship with her mother-in-law; and the problems generated by her four sons, James, Elliott, Franklin, Jr., and John, her daughter, Anna, and her brother Hall.

Eleanor built Val-Kill partly as a retreat from her mother-in-law, who autocratically ruled the family from Springwood, the "Big House" some two miles distant. The idea of building a structure at Val-Kill emerged in 1924 at a picnic attended by Eleanor, her husband, and Eleanor's friends Nancy Cook and Marion Dickerman. Roosevelt offered the three women a life interest in the property. They constructed a "Dutch colonial" cottage of fieldstone designed by Henry Toombs; FDR, who had an intense interest in vernacular Hudson Valley architecture, provided much design advice. The design included a rustic pool for swimming and a formal, walled garden attached to the cottage. The site was named Val-Kill, a name created by the Roosevelt family; the Fall-Kill was the historic name of the stream running through the property.

The original stone cottage designed by FDR and architect Henry Toombs overlooks a pond created by impounding the water of the Fall-Kill, which flows through the property. The word *Kill* means stream or brook in Dutch. Photo: Richard Pileggi, 1997, for Historic Hudson Valley.

An endless stream of people associated with Eleanor Roosevelt's many causes made pilgrimages to Val-Kill. Here she is pictured in the company of visitors from UNESCO, at Val-Kill, July, 1948. President Truman first appointed Eleanor to the United States delegation to the United Nations, where she served in a number of capacities with great distinction. At her feet is Fala, the Scottish terrier given to FDR by Margaret Suckley. Fala became the most famous of all presidential dogs. At FDR's death, Fala went back to Wilderstein with Miss Suckley, but presently returned to Val-Kill to live with Eleanor at the Roosevelt family's request. Photo: FDR Library, Hyde Park.

Eleanor used Val-Kill whenever she was at Hyde Park and spent the nights there when FDR was absent from Springwood. It became her refuge, where she found stimulating companionship, self-fulfillment, and independence.

In 1926, Eleanor, Marion, and Nancy, joined by a third friend, Caroline O'Day, became business partners in a furniture and metalwork factory close by the Stone Cottage. The purpose of Val-Kill Industries, as it was called, was to train young men of the Hyde Park community, especially farmers, in a craft that would give them an additional source of income. The business operated until 1936, when it lost its market and folded. Then Eleanor converted the factory into apartments for herself and her secretary, Malvina ("Tommy") Thompson, and the factory became Val-Kill Cottage.

Improvements to Val-Kill were made through the years, including the artificial seven-acre pond (circa 1925), outdoor fireplace (1933), a modern, heated swimming pool (1935), tennis court (1950), and rose garden (1960).

Val-Kill was continually filled with family and guests, including personal friends of the Roosevelts, and groups and organizations in which Eleanor had a personal interest. FDR enjoyed exercising in the pool and attending cookouts and picnics on the grounds but did not sleep there. Occasionally, during their Presidential years, the Roosevelts entertained state visitors at Val-Kill, among them King George VI and Queen Elizabeth. (The celebrated and much publicized royal picnic of 1939 was held at the President's own retreat, Top Cottage, which he designed and built that year on a hill adjacent to Val-Kill.

This historic dwelling is expected to be open to the public in the near future.)

After FDR's death in 1945, Eleanor was able to purchase the house and about 1,000 acres from her husband's estate. In 1947, she bought out Nancy Cook and Marion Dickerman, from whom she had become estranged. She and her son Elliott immediately began Val-Kill Farms, which operated for a short time and had limited success as a business venture.

Because Eleanor and her children had disclaimed their life interest in Springwood, which FDR had left to the Federal government, Val-Kill became the center of, rather than a retreat from, the Roosevelt family at Hyde Park. Eleanor made Val-Kill the place for family functions and, in effect, a small conference center where she hosted meetings for the many causes in which she was involved. Val-Kill was also where Eleanor entertained a wide range of world leaders and dignitaries, among them Ethiopian Emperor Haile Selassie, Soviet leader Nikita Khrushchev, Yugoslavian dictator Marshal Tito, Prime Minister of India Jawaharlal Nehru, labor leader Walter Reuther, and Democratic party presidential candidates Adlai Stevenson and John F. Kennedy.

Eleanor Roosevelt died in 1962 and was buried next to her husband in the rose garden at Springwood. Their son John A. Roosevelt (1916–1981) owned Val-Kill, converted Val-Kill Cottage into four rental units, resided in the Stone Cottage, and eventually sold the property. Through the efforts of a non-profit community-based organization known as the Eleanor Roosevelt Center at Val-Kill, however, the site was purchased by the Federal government in 1977 and made into a National Historic Site. It was dedicated and opened to the public in 1984.

VAL-KILL
A National Historic Site (1977)
National Park Service
Roosevelt-Vanderbilt National Historic Sites
Hyde Park, NY 12538
Telephone: 914/229-9422
Fax: 914/229-0739
e-mail: *ROVA_webmaster@nps.gov*
Internet: *www.nps.gov/ELR*
Open daily from April through October;
open weekends from November through March.
9am–5pm.
Trails, special events.
Entrance on Rt. 9G, north of intersection with
St. Andrews Road.

Eleanor Roosevelt poses at Val-Kill with three of her granddaughters. "Her innate austerity," wrote her son Elliott, "made it impossible for her to gush over [her grandchildren], but they knew how much she cared." She had over thirty grandchildren and great grandchildren, to whom she wrote volumes of letters and cards and sent generous gifts on birthdays, at Christmas, and on other important occasions. Photo: FDR Library, Hyde Park.

The U-shaped east front of the FDR Library today, showing the building very much as it appeared in 1941. (The wings FDR included in his proposal, which were built in 1972, are not visible in this photograph.) The "Dutch Colonial" elements in the design include the irregular fieldstone walls, shed dormer windows, and engaged, one-story porches. Photo: Richard Pileggi, 1997, for Historic Hudson Valley.

FDR LIBRARY & MUSEUM

NATIONAL ARCHIVES AND RECORDS ADMINISTRATION ✳ HYDE PARK

The records which will be collected here are the records, in this precise and common sense, of an era and a time.
They are the records of a period in which the strong and restless life of the American people refused to accept the world
as it had been and demanded that the world become the world their longing could imagine. They are the records of the speaking
and the action of a man who, more than any other man, has been the actor and the speaker of this time—the man who refused,
in the name of his generation, to continue to accept what was no longer acceptable—the man who demanded, for his generation,
what his generation had the courage to demand. As such they have the unity which history remembers and even living
men can see. They belong by themselves, here in this river country, on the land from which they came.

—ARCHIBALD MACLEISH, 1939, THE LIBRARIAN OF CONGRESS

I have destroyed practically nothing. As a result, we have a mine for which future historians will curse as well as
praise me. It is a mine which will need to have the dross sifted from the gold. I would like to do it but I am informed by the
professors that I am not capable of doing it. They even admit that they are not capable of doing it. They say that they must
wait for that dim, distant period . . . when the definitive history of this particular era will come to be written.

—FRANKLIN D. ROOSEVELT, 1939

Created originally as an architectural and functional extension of the Springwood estate, the FDR Library was the first Presidential Library and Museum. It reflects in a personal and affecting way the life and career of one of the greatest presidents in American history and the momentous times that coincided with his administration. The Library also contains the papers of Eleanor Roosevelt, whose own influence and achievements place her in the pantheon of great Americans, quite apart from her role as First Lady.

As Franklin D. Roosevelt (1882–1945) neared the end of his second and what he most likely presumed would be his last term in the White House, he began to consider his retirement plans and the disposition of his personal and political papers. Beginning with George Washington, Presidents had taken their papers with them, treating them as their personal property and disposing of them more or less as they pleased. Certain of his place in history and concerned that the documentary legacy of his life and times and his treasured collections of books and memorabilia might be dispersed, Roosevelt decided to build a library at Hyde Park. Extensive consultation on the project involved the National Archives and many of the most eminent historians of the time, led by Samuel Eliot Morison. Their involvement was in part designed to deflect the understandable criticism that FDR was trying to build his own memorial.

This room replaced the small office in the main house that FDR used while visiting Springwood. The portrait of Sara Delano Roosevelt, her gift to Franklin, was painted by Douglas Chandor in 1940 for this room. The room appears just as FDR left it on his last visit on March 28, 1945. Photo: Mick Hales, 1997, for Historic Hudson Valley.

The unprecedented idea of building a presidential library dedicated to a single President's administration had its detractors, to be sure. One called it a "pyramid;" another thought it a clear reflection of FDR's "egotistical, incompetent, unscrupulous, and unspeakably costly administration." Nevertheless, every President after Roosevelt has enthusiastically followed suit with a library of his own.

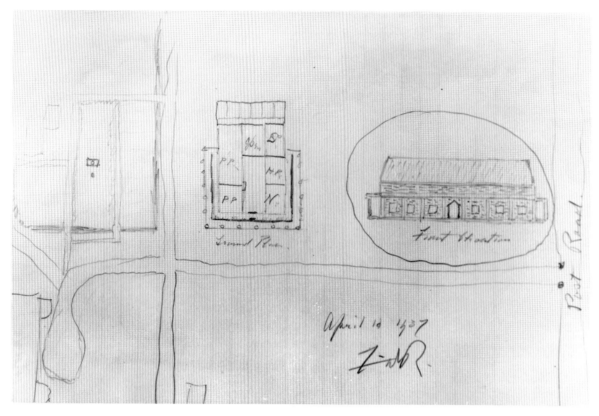

First sketch (April, 1937) for a site plan, floor plans, and elevations in Franklin Roosevelt's hand. The "big house" is at lower left, above which is the rose garden and future location of FDR's and Eleanor Roosevelt's graves. The placement of the library at the entrance, close to the road, turned the existing compound of house, garden, and domestic service buildings into something FDR clearly intended as a memorial to his life and administration. Collection of the FDR Library, Hyde Park.

At the same time, Roosevelt completed plans in his favorite "Dutch Colonial" style for a small retirement retreat near Val-Kill, which he called Top Cottage. No doubt he planned to retire to Hyde Park, live at Springwood, write his memoirs using his papers and the resources of the Library, and spend private time at Top Cottage very much as Eleanor used Val-Kill. FDR not only intended the Library to be a repository for his Federal and State papers, but also for personal material, including collections of books and memorabilia relating to the Hudson River Valley and local Dutchess County history, subjects in which he was immensely interested. This is why FDR expected the Library to be a meeting place for the region's historical societies and other like-minded associations.

FDR (and his mother, begrudgingly) contributed about sixteen acres of land a short distance from the house for the Library, and FDR conceived the slate-roofed, "Dutch Colonial" style fieldstone building, incorporating a spacious, well-appointed office for his personal use. Built by private subscription at a cost of approximately $375,000, from designs by Henry Toombs (who designed

FDR's Warms Springs, Georgia compound, Val-Kill for Eleanor in the 1920s, and Top Cottage for FDR in the late 1930s), the building was completed and turned over the Federal government in 1940, the year before his mother's death. The museum was opened to the public in 1941, with an entrance fee of 25 cents covering maintenance. FDR's "closest companion" and distant cousin Margaret ("Daisy") Suckley of Wilderstein joined the staff as a part-time junior archivist. In 1942, Roosevelt sketched designs for the north and south wings.

President Roosevelt did not retire after his second term, but won unprecedented third and fourth terms. This postponed his retirement plans and his own intended use of the Library. During Roosevelt's third and fourth terms, the Georgian Revival-style study in the building became his office away from the White House, the scene of conferences with state visitors, and the site of four of his "fireside chat" radio broadcasts. No other Presidential library has ever been used by the Chief Executive during his presidency.

After Roosevelt's death, the Library resources continued to expand. The wings originally sketched by Roosevelt

FDR (October, 1938) is seated in his car behind Top Cottage, the retreat he was building on his Hyde Park estate. The fieldstone cottage was completed the next year to FDR's own designs, with the assistance of architect Henry Toombs. The cottage accommodated the President's wheelchair and his needs on one level. FDR's aging mother, dismayed that he would want to be away from her at Springwood, extracted a promise that FDR would never spend a night here as long as she lived. Photo: FDR Library, Hyde Park.

thirty years earlier were constructed in 1972 to provide enlarged research facilities and a gallery interpreting the life of Eleanor Roosevelt. Her papers, amounting to an astonishing three million pages, were deposited in the Library. In addition to its manuscripts, the Library holds large collections of books, photographs, recordings, film, memorabilia, and the papers of several of FDR's key political associates, including Harry Hopkins and Henry Morgenthau, Jr.

The establishment of the Franklin D. Roosevelt Library significantly changed the protocol for the disposition of presidential papers and started the presidential library system that exists today. Because the Library opened to scholars a massive volume of primary research material, it also changed research methods and accelerated the pace of contemporary history writing. Perhaps most importantly, the professional, scholarly approach to the preservation of presidential papers, recordings, and other material tended to de-politicize Federal archival procedures. The changes initiated by the Roosevelt administration in the way presidential documents were treated prompted Archivist of the United States Robert D.W.

Conner to describe FDR in 1941 as "the nation's answer to the historian's prayer." Today the Library is an important research center for scholars, with museum exhibits handsomely reinstalled in recent years.

FDR LIBRARY & MUSEUM

The National Archives and Records Administration
511 Albany Post Road
Hyde Park, NY 12538
Telephone: 914/229-8114
or 1-800-FDR-VISIT
Fax: 914/229-0872
e-mail: *library@roosevelt.nara.gov*
Website: *www.nara.gov*
Open daily except Thanksgiving, Christmas, and New Year's Day 9am–6pm.
Exhibition galleries, Museum Shop, research library.
Driving directions: Located on Rt. 9 (Albany Post Rd.) at the south end of Hyde Park, on the grounds of Springwood, the Roosevelt estate.

Selected Bibliography

Adams, Arthur G., *The Hudson Through The Years*. Lind Publications, Westwood, NJ, 1983.

The Architecture of McKim, Mead & White. With an introduction by Richard Guy Wilson. New York: Dover Publications, Inc., 1990.

William Alex, *Calvert Vaux, Architect and Planner*. New York: Ink, Inc., 1994.

Clive Aslet, *The American Country House*. New Haven: Yale University Press, 1990.

William Lawrence Bottomley, chairman, Architects Emergency Committee, *Great Georgian Houses of America*, Vol. 2, 1937. New York: Dover Publications, 1970.

Clare Brandt, *An American Aristocracy: The Livingstons*. New York: Doubleday, 1986.

Fredrika Bremer, *The Homes of the New World*. New York: Harper & Brothers, 1853.

Joseph T. Butler, "Montgomery Place Revisited." The Magazine *Antiques*. August, 1988. p. 295–303.

Gerald Carr, *Olana Landscape*. New York: Rizzoli, 1989.

A. James Casner and W. Barton Leach, *Cases and Text on Property*. 2nd edition. Boston: Little, Brown and Co., 1969.

Thomas Streatfeild Clarkson, *A Biographical History of Clermont or Livingston Manor*. Privately published: Clermont, 1869.

George Dangerfield, *Chancellor Robert R. Livingston of New York 1746–1813*. New York: Harcourt, Brace, & Co., 1960.

Alexander Jackson Davis, *Rural Residences, etc*. New York, 1837. (The book was reprinted by Da Capo Press in 1979.)

Howland Davis and Arthur Kelly (compilers), *A Livingston Genealogical Register*. Clermont, NY: Friends of Clermont, 1995.

John Ross Delafield, "Montgomery Place." Dutchess County Historical Society Yearbook, 1929, pp. 26–31.

Anita K. Delafield, "Living With Antiques: Montgomery Place, the Home of Major and Mrs. John White Delafield." The Magazine *Antiques*, February, 1967. Vol. 91, pp. 234–9.

Julia Livingston Delafield, *Biographies of Francis Lewis and Morgan Lewis*. New York: Randolph & Co., 1877.

Harold Donaldson Eberlein and Cortlandt Van Dyke Hubbard, *Historic Houses of the Hudson Valley*. New York: Dover Publications, 1990. (A reprint of the original edition, 1942).

A.J. Downing, *Landscape Gardening and Rural Architecture*. New York: Dover Publications, 1991. (A reprint of the 7th edition, 1865.)

A. J. Downing, *A Treatise on the Theory and Practice of Landscape Gardening, Adapted to North America*. New York: Wiley and Putnam, 1844. (2nd edition.)

Olin Dows, *Franklin Roosevelt at Hyde Park*. New York: American Artists Group, 1949.

John Foreman and Robbe Pierce Stimson, *The Vanderbilts and the Gilded Age*. New York: St. Martin's Press, 1991.

Doris Kearns Goodwin, *No Ordinary Time*. New York: Touchstone, 1995.

Jacquetta M. Haley, "Montgomery Place, A History of Place and People." Unpublished manuscript, Historic Hudson Valley, 1988.

Jacquetta M. Haley, *Pleasure Grounds: Andrew Jackson Downing and Montgomery Place*. Tarrytown: Sleepy Hollow Press, 1988.

William B. Hatcher, *Edward Livingston: Jeffersonian Republican and Jacksonian Democrat*. Baton Rouge: Louisiana State University Press, 1940.

John K. Howat, *The Hudson River And Its Painters*. New York: Penguin, 1972.

Mark Alan Hewitt, *The Architect and the American Country House 1890–1940*. New Haven: Yale University Press, 1990.

David C. Huntington, *The Landscapes of Frederic Edwin Church*. New York: George Braziller, 1966.

Kathleen Eagen Johnson and Timothy Steinhoff, *Art of the Landscape: Sunnyside, Montgomery Place, and Romanticism*. Tarrytown: Historic Hudson Valley Press, 1997.

Franklin Kelly, Stephen J. Gould, and James A. Ryan, *Frederic Edwin Church*. Washington: National Gallery of Art and Smithsonian Press, 1989.

Cynthia A. Kierner, *Traders and Gentlefolk, The Livingstons of New York, 1675–1790*. Ithaca: Cornell University Press, 1992.

Sung Bok Kim, *Landlord and Tenant in Colonial New York: Manorial Society, 1664–1775*. Institute of Early American History and Culture, Williamsburg, Virginia. Chapel Hill: University of North Carolina Press, 1978.

Francis R. Kowsky, *Country, Park, and City: The Architecture and Life of Calvert Vaux, 1824–1895*. Oxford University Press, 1997.

John Brett Langstaff, *Doctor Bard of Hyde Park*. New York: E.P. Dutton & Co., 1942.

Joseph P. Lash, *Eleanor & Franklin*. New York: Norton & Company, 1971.

Edwin Brockholst Livingston, *The Livingstons of Livingston Manor*. The Knickerbocker Press, 1910.

John Henry Livingston, "The Livingston Manor." The Order of Colonial Lords of Manors in America, privately printed for the Order in pamphlet form (first in a series), New York, 1914.

Benson J. Lossing, *The Hudson, from the Wilderness to the Sea.* New York: Virtue & Yorston, 1866.

Carleton Mabee, *The American Leonardo, A Life of Samuel F.B. Morse.* New York: Alfred A. Knopf, 1943.

Robert B. MacKay, Anthony Baker, and Carol A. Traynor, editors, *Long Island Country Houses and Their Architects.* New York: W.W. Norton & Co., 1997.

Judith K. Major, *To Live in the New World: A.J. Downing and American Landscape Gardening.* Cambridge: MIT Press, 1997.

Mesick, Cohen, and Waite, Architects, *Wilderstein Historic Structures Report.* Wilderstein Preservation: 1992.

Metropolitan Museum of Art, *In Pursuit of Beauty.* New York: Metropolitan Museum of Art, 1986.

National Park Service, brochures for the Vanderbilt Mansion, Springwood, and Val-Kill.

Julian Ursyn Niemcewicz, *Under Their Vine and Fig Tree: Travels through America in 1797–1799, 1805, with some further account of life in New Jersey.* Translated and edited by Metchie J. E. Budka. Vol. XIV, Collections of The New Jersey Historical Society at Newark, 1965.

Patricia M. O'Donnell, Charles A. Birnbaum, and Cynthia Zaitzevsky, *Cultural Landscape Report for Vanderbilt Mansion National Historic Site.* Boston: The National Park Service, 1992.

Amelia Peck (editor), *Alexander Jackson Davis: American Architect, 1803–1892.* New York: Rizzoli, 1992.

Cynthia Owen Philip, "Wilderstein: The Creation of a Hudson River Villa, 1852–1897." *The Hudson Valley Regional Review*, September, 1990, Vol. 7, #2, pp. 1–60.

Ruth Piwonka, *A Portrait of Livingston Manor.* Friends of Clermont, 1986.

Ruth Piwonka and Roderic H. Blackburn, *A Visible Heritage: Columbia County, New York.* Black Dome Press, 1996.

Helen Wilkinson Reynolds, "The Story of Locust Grove," Dutchess County Historical Society Yearbook, 1932, pp. 21–32.

Helen Wilkinson Reynolds, *Dutchess County Doorways.* New York: William Farquhar Payson, 1931.

Christine Chapman Robbins, *David Hosack, Citizen of New York.* Philadelphia: The American Philosophical Society, 1964.

Eleanor Roosevelt, *This I Remember.* New York: Harper & Brothers, 1949.

Elliott Roosevelt and James Brough, *The Roosevelts of the White House: A Rendezvous with Destiny.* New York: G. P. Putnam's Sons, 1975.

Julia Schaller Ross, *Montgomery Place: The Twentieth Century Gardens.* Tarrytown: Historic Hudson Valley, 1988.

David Schuyler, *Apostle of Taste: Andrew Jackson Downing, 1815–1952.* Baltimore: Johns Hopkins University Press, 1996.

Joel E. Spingarn, "Henry Winthrop Sargent and the early history of landscape gardening and ornamental horticulture in Dutchess County, New York." Dutchess County Historical Society Yearbook, 1937, pp. 36–70. Also appeared as "Henry Winthrop Sargent and the Landscape Tradition at Wodenethe" in the Oct. 1938 issue of *Landscape Architecture* magazine.

Clara and Hardy Steeholm, *The House at Hyde Park, together with Sara Delano Roosevelt's Household Book.* New York: Viking Press, 1950.

Adam Sweeting, *Reading Houses and Building Books.* Hanover: University Press of New England, 1996.

Sari B. Tietjen, *Rhinebeck, Portrait of a Town.* Rhinebeck: Phanter Press, 1990

Robert M. Toole, *Historic Landscape Report/Olana State Historic Site.* New York State Office of Parks, Recreation, and Historic Preservation, 1996.

United States Coast and Geodetic Survey, *Atlantic Coast Local Pilot Subdivision 13,* 2nd edition. Washington: US Government Printing Office, 1880.

Calvert Vaux, *Villas and Cottages.* New York: Dover Publications, 1970.

Geoffrey C. Ward, *Before the Trumpet: Young Franklin Roosevelt 1882–1905.* New York: Harper & Row, 1985.

Geoffrey C. Ward, *A First Class Temperament: the Emergence of Franklin Roosevelt.* New York: Harper & Row, 1989.

Geoffrey C. Ward, editor, *Closest Companion: The Unknown Story of the Intimate Friendship between Franklin Roosevelt and Margaret Suckley.* Boston: Houghton Mifflin, 1995.

Geoffrey C. Ward, "Future Historians Will Curse As Well As Praise Me." *Smithsonian* Magazine, December, 1989: p. 58–69.

John Zukowsky and Robbe Pierce Stimson, *Hudson River Villas.* New York: Rizzoli, 1985.

ACKNOWLEDGMENTS

Major funding for this project was generously provided by Furthermore, the publication program of The J.M. Kaplan Fund. Additional funding was provided by the Greenway Conservancy of the Hudson River Valley, Inc., Dutchess County Tourism, the Eleanor and Franklin Roosevelt Institute, the FDR Library in Hyde Park, and the Samuel F. B. Morse Historic Site. The project also benefited materially from the support of Governor George E. Pataki.

This project was organized by Historic Hudson Valley and completed with the cooperation of staff members of all the museum properties included in the text. Skip Cole, Superintendent of the Roosevelt-Vanderbilt Sites of the National Park Service; James Moogan, Regional Director, and Dennis Wentworth, Regional Director of Operations, New York State Office of Parks, Recreation, and Historic Preservation; and Lucy Kuriger, Site Director, Montgomery Place served on the planning committee.

In addition to writing the introduction, J. Winthrop Aldrich provided endless support, superb advice, and very detailed comments. This guide would have been filled with errors without his scholarly eye and depth of knowledge.

Burns Patterson planned and supervised the photography. Portions of the text were initially drafted and reviewed by Bruce Naramore (Clermont), Sally Dann (Locust Grove), James Ryan (Olana), Scott Rector and Fran Macsali (Springwood and Val-Kill), Allan Daily (Hyde Park), Patricia Weber (Wilderstein), and Melodye Moore (Staatsburgh). The FDR Library staff and the office of Verne Newton provided detailed information; Lynn Bassanese read the FDR Library entry and made corrections. Valuable editorial comments, information, and assistance were supplied by Ray Armater, Thomas Basile, Kelly Bazemore, Thomas Brener, Kathleen Casey, Anne Ricard Cassidy, Susan Cavanaugh, Kathryn Coulam, Joan K. Davidson, John H. Dobkin, Robert Engel, Toni Giglio, Susan Greenstein, Sara Johns Griffen, Renee Nisivoccia, Ross Higgins, Kathleen Eagen Johnson, Anne Jordan, Joan Martin, Eleanor McBride, Scott McCloud, Scott Marshall, Al Moskowitz, Cindy Nielsen, Austin O'Brien, Dolores LaCarrubba, Eugenia Pakalik, Burns Patterson, Mark Renovitch, Karen Sharman, Diana D. Smith, Kenneth F. Snodgrass, Timothy Steinhoff, Waddell Stillman, Jill Taylor, Raymond Teichman, Bill Urbin, Margaret Vetare, Mary Kay Vrba, Duane Watson, Linda Watson, Karen Woods, and Karen Zukowski.

Photographic credits are included in the picture captions. Special thanks are due to Richard Pileggi, a professional photographer who generously contributed his talents. Steven Schoenfelder designed this publication, and Robert Romagnoli made the maps for the Historic Hudson Valley Press.